How to Use Your Dictionary

Fun Activities for Students Learning Dictionary and Thesaurus Skills

Mary Wood Cornog, Ph.D. and The Editors of Merriam-Webster Inc.

Merriam-Webster, Incorporated
Springfield, Massachusetts

A GENUINE MERRIAM-WEBSTER

The name *Webster* alone is no guarantee of excellence. It is used by a number of publishers and may serve to mislead an unwary buyer.

Merriam-Webster™ is the name you should look for when you consider the purchase of dictionaries or other fine reference books. It carries the reputation of a company that has been publishing since 1831 and is your assurance of quality and authority.

Copyright © 2004 by Merriam-Webster, Incorporated

All rights reserved.

Limited Reproduction Permission. The purchase of this unit entitles the individual teacher to reproduce copies for classroom use. Reproduction of any part of this book for an entire school or school system is strictly prohibited.

ISBN 0-87779-670-X

Text and cover design by Lynn Stowe Tomb
Editorial assistance from Rebecca Bryer and Kara Noble

Printed in the United States of America
04 05 06 07   QWD   5 4 3 2 1

Contents

For the Teacher	4a
Learning Objectives	5a
Tips for Teachers	6a
Introduction to the Dictionary	**7a**
What is a Dictionary?	8a
How Does a Word Get in the Dictionary?	9a
Who Was Noah Webster?	11a
How to Use Your Dictionary	**1**
1. Alphabetical Order—Getting Started	3
2. Alphabetical Order—Moving Along	5
3. Guide Words	7
4. End-of-Line Divisions	9
5. Pronunciation	11
6. More About Pronunciation	13
7. Still More About Pronunciation	15
8. Variants	17
9. Functional Labels	19
10. Homographs	21
11. Inflected Forms	23
12. Usage Labels	25
13. Definitions—Meaning	27
14. Definitions—Historical Order	29
15. Synonyms and Cross-references	31
16. Verbal Illustrations	33
17. Usage Notes	35
18. Undefined Entries	37
19. Synonym Paragraphs	39
20. Phrases	41
21. Word History Paragraphs	43
How to Use Your Thesaurus	**45**
22. What Is a Thesaurus?	47
23. Meaning Cores and Verbal Illustrations	49
24. Synonyms and Related Words	51
25. Phrases	53
26. Antonyms and Near Antonyms	55
Vocabulary Building Exercises	**57**
Answer Key	**74**

© 2004 Merriam-Webster Inc.

For the Teacher

Introduction

The ability to use reference resources effectively is essential to establishing the strong communication skills needed to succeed in today's complex world. The purpose of this book is to introduce students to the dictionary and thesaurus, to explain their contents, and to put students at ease with the typographical and structural conventions of these resources. As a result, students will come to use their dictionary and thesaurus easily and confidently to improve and develop their reading, writing and speaking.

This book is designed for students in grades 4-7. Examples provided throughout the text demonstrate and clarify the concepts presented. The exercises cover a variety of question types, including multiple choice, matching, cloze, and short writing prompts, to allow students to practice new skills and demonstrate mastery in various ways. Vocabulary-building activities at the back of the book encourage students to expand their vocabulary in entertaining and creative explorations of words and language.

Organization of this book

1. Introductory material for the teacher—This section includes valuable information about the structure of the book, teaching and assessment tips, and a table correlating the lessons in the book to curriculum and assessment guidelines and standards as established by national organizations of educators and selected state educational agencies.

2. Introductory material for the student—This section contains an introduction to dictionaries, plus two enrichment pages that include writing activities that can be completed individually or in groups. It is recommended that students read the *What is a Dictionary?* page before beginning the lessons. The enrichment pages may be used before beginning the lessons or can be interspersed where desired as student move through the lessons.

3. Lessons—Each of the 26 lessons in this book includes explanatory text that describes and explains a feature of the dictionary or thesaurus that includes illustrative examples demonstrating the elements and concepts presented. Exercises follow that allow students to apply newly learned skills and information. Lessons are on perforated pages that may be removed from the book, or the teacher may photocopy lesson pages if desired. The lessons in this book were developed from *Merriam-Webster's Elementary Dictionary, Merriam-Webster's Intermediate Dictionary,* and *Merriam-Webster's Intermediate Thesaurus.* Students should be able to successfully complete all activities in the lessons in this book using those references.

4. Vocabulary building activities—The vocabulary-building section includes enrichment activities intended to be fun and challenging for students. Each activity page includes three questions that can be answered by looking up words or other information in the dictionary. All end with an open-ended writing activity that can be answered by looking up the word history information in *Merriam-Webster's Intermediate Dictionary* or on Merriam-Webster's student Web site, WordCentral.com.

5. Answer keys—The answer keys list correct responses for the activities in the lessons and in the vocabulary building activities. Where appropriate, enrichment material is provided to enable the teacher to expand upon basic answers.

Learning Objectives

The following learning objectives meet curriculum and assessment guidelines as established by national organizations of educators, including National Council of Teachers of English and the International Reading Association and selected state educational agencies.

Learning Objective	Chapter
1. Interpret information in dictionaries, thesauruses, and other reliable reference sources.	All
2. Apply knowledge of alphabetization to successfully locate information in reference sources.	1-3
3. Understand sound-letter correspondences and word and language structure, and apply that knowledge to decode words.	5, 6, 7, 10, 11
4. Understand and apply conventions for grammar, capitalization, punctuation, and spelling in English.	4, 9, 11, 12, 16, 17
5. Understand and apply conventions of English usage.	9, 11, 12, 13, 14, 16, 17, 20
6. Recognize and apply correct spellings for English words, including commonly misspelled words.	1, 2, 8, 9
7. Apply structural analysis of words, including an understanding of root words, inflected forms, and affixes, to decode meaning and interpret texts.	7, 11, 18
8. Demonstrate an understanding of the diversity of word meaning, pronunciations, and spelling in English.	7, 8, 9, 10, 13
9. Understand and apply knowledge of a broad range of words and phrases from a variety of disciplines.	All
10. Differentiate among words of similar or related meaning, including synonyms, antonyms, related and contrasted words, and idioms.	10, 13, 15, 16, 18, 19, 20, 22, 23, 24, 25, 26
11. Understand and use homophones and homographs correctly.	5, 6, 7, 10
12. Use word origins to enrich understanding of the influences of other cultures and languages on English words.	14, 21
13. Read and write words, phrases, and idioms in a variety of texts and contexts, using references to enhance word choice, self-editing, and proofreading.	All

© 2004 Merriam-Webster Inc.

Tips for Teachers

- Lessons can be completed individually, in small groups, or as a class activity.

- If students complete lessons independently, have them read the explanatory information first, then answer the questions. If done as a class or small group activity, discuss the examples in the text with the students and encourage them to talk to each other about it.

- Encourage students to do some of the written exercises, especially the open-ended writing exercises, in groups and to work as a team to find answers.

- Encourage students to look up examples from the lessons and compare actual dictionary entries with the lesson examples.

- When words have multiple meanings, have students discuss how the meanings are similar and different. When they reach the lesson on historical order of definitions (Chapter 14), encourage them to discuss how the meaning of a word has changed over time.

- Have students keep a word inventory, either on cards or in their notebook or journal, to keep track of the new words they learn in each lesson. Encourage them to make lists of words they already know, words they have seen but don't really know, and words that are new to them in the lesson.

- Have students write original sentences to illustrate vocabulary words in their notebook or journal.

- Have students compare entries in the dictionary and thesaurus and talk about how each type of entry helps them understand a word better.

- If students use varying pronunciations, encourage them to check the pronunciations in the dictionary. Discuss the fact that pronunciations can vary by geographic region.

- Encourage students to look up words in online dictionaries, such as the one at WordCentral.com. Have them compare online dictionary entries to those in the printed dictionary. *Note:* The dictionary at WordCentral.com is *Merriam-Webster's Intermediate Dictionary*.

- Have them write the answers to the "Words in Action" exercises in a notebook or journal so they can build a writing portfolio. Keeping answers in the same place can also aid in reviewing lessons and vocabulary.

- "Words in Action" pieces are designed to be open-ended and to encourage students to respond creatively. There is no single "right" answer. In assessing student writing, consider whether they follow instructions, whether their writing demonstrates improvement in their overall skill level, how well they apply the techniques and information presented in the lesson, and the effort and creativity they put into developing their response.

- Have students read and edit each other's writing activity answers. Encourage them to use constructive criticism and to point out strong points in the writing as well as aspects that need revision.

- Use "Words in Action," "Word Workout," and "Word History Detective" exercises as enrichment activities interspersed throughout your study of the dictionary.

Introduction to the Dictionary

What is a Dictionary?

Wouldn't it be great to have a book that could help you write better? One that could help you make sure you say things the right way? A book that makes it easier to read other books, magazines, and newspapers? One that would tell you how to use words properly? You probably already have that book. It's called your dictionary.

A dictionary is a reference book that contains a list of words, usually in alphabetical order. It also includes information about word meanings, pronunciations, functions, histories, and uses. You are probably most familiar with dictionaries that are printed as books, such as *Merriam-Webster's Elementary Dictionary* or *Merriam-Webster's Intermediate Dictionary*. However, not all dictionaries are printed. They can also be found on computers, on CD-ROMs, and on the World Wide Web.

Whether your dictionary is in a book or on a computer, you will find it has some special features. One thing you'll probably notice right away is that some words in the dictionary are printed in **boldface** type. Other words are printed in small capital letters (like this: INSTANCE), and some parts of the dictionary entry are printed in slanted *italic* type. You'll see backward slash marks with strange characters between them (\ig-ˈzam-pəl\), and short phrases marked off by pointed brackets (called *angle brackets*), like these ⟨ ⟩. You'll see numbers and colons (:). You'll even see pictures.

Knowing what all those features mean is the key to making the dictionary work for you. Once you understand the rules that dictionaries use, you can use your dictionary to help you understand the meaning of words. Your dictionary can guide you in spelling and pronouncing words. It can teach you how to use words correctly. It can tell you the differences between words that have similar meanings. And it can let you explore the fascinating histories of words, learning where they came from and why we started using them.

Sometimes, the best way to understand what a word means is to see a picture of the thing it names—so dictionaries also have pictures. The dictionary also includes hundreds of example phrases and sentences. They show how words are actually used in speech and writing.

newt

All of this can be a bit confusing, especially if you are new to using dictionaries. But don't worry. The purpose of this book is to help you understand all the funny-looking characters and print types in the dictionary. The lessons in it will help you to unlock the treasure trove of information in the dictionary and learn how to use it to improve your daily reading, writing, and speaking.

How Does a Word Get into the Dictionary?

"How does a word get into the dictionary?' That's a question people often ask. The answer is simple: Words get into the dictionary because people use them.

It's actually a little more complicated than that, but not much. In general, in order for a word to be entered in the dictionary, it must appear regularly in books, magazines, or newspapers. To decide which words to include in the dictionary and to determine what they mean, dictionary editors, like those at Merriam-Webster, study the language to determine which words people use most often and how they use them.

Merriam-Webster editors spend part of each day reading books, newspapers, magazines, and electronic publications—a sampling of all kinds of published materials. At Merriam-Webster, this activity is called "reading and marking." The editors are looking for examples of new words, new meanings of existing words, evidence of different spellings—anything that might help in deciding if a word belongs in the dictionary and what it means. Any word of interest is marked, along with surrounding text that shows how the word is used and what it means. The marked passages are then input into a computer system and stored both in the computer and on 3" x 5" slips of paper. These passages are called *citations*.

Each citation has the following elements:
1. the word itself
2. an example of the word used in context
3. information about the publication from which the word and example were taken

Merriam-Webster's citation files, which were begun in the 1880s, now contain nearly 15 million citations. Citations are also available to editors in a text database (language experts call it a *corpus*) that includes 70 million words drawn from a wide variety of publications.

How does a word make the jump from the citation file to the dictionary? How do editors decide they have enough citations to put the word in the dictionary?

The process begins with a dictionary editor called a *definer*. Definers start by looking at citations covering a small section of the alphabet—for example, words beginning *gri-* —along with the entries from the dictionary that are included within that alphabetical section. The definer's job is to decide which entries can remain unchanged, which entries need to be revised, which entries can be dropped, and which new entries should be added. In each case, the definer decides on the best course of action by reading citations and then adjusting the entries or creating new ones to match the evidence in the citations.

© 2004 Merriam-Webster Inc.

Before a new word can be added to the dictionary, it must have enough citations to show that it is widely used. But having a lot of citations is not enough. A word may be rejected for entry into a general dictionary if all of its citations come from a single publication or if they are all from highly specialized publications that reflect the special vocabulary of experts within a single field.

To be included in a Merriam-Webster dictionary, a word must be used in citations that come from a wide range of publications over a considerable period of time. Specifically, the word must have enough citations to allow accurate judgments about its frequency of use, currency, and meaning.

The size and type of dictionary affect how many citations a word needs to gain admission. Because an abridged dictionary, such as *Merriam-Webster's Elementry Dictionary* or even *Merriam-Webster's Collegiate® Dictionary, Eleventh Edition,* has fairly limited space, only the most commonly used words can be entered. To get into that type of dictionary, a word must be supported by a significant number of citations. But a large unabridged dictionary, such as *Webster's Third New International Dictionary,* has room for many more words, so terms with fewer citations can still be included.

Change and variation are as natural in language as they are in other areas of human life, and good dictionaries must reflect that fact. By relying on evidence of actual use, Merriam-Webster editors keep their dictionaries up-to-date and accurate. In that way, Merriam-Webster dictionaries speak with authority and fulfill their mission to tell the truth about words.

Words in Action

Here's your chance to be an English inventor! Make up a new, original word. Design an advertisement for your word that will encourage people to use it.

Web Field Trip

Go to Merriam-Webster's WordCentral Web site at http://www.wordcentral.com and click on the **Build Your Own Dictionary** link. Submit your new word to WordCentral's online student dictionary.

© 2004 Merriam-Webster Inc.

Who Was Noah Webster?

Noah Webster was born in West Hartford, Connecticut, in 1758 and grew up in the years just before the American Revolution. He was a active supporter of the new nation and a strong believer in the value of education for its citizens. He is most famous for writing the first American dictionary, which showed that the country had its own brand of English with its own vocabulary, pronunciation, and spelling.

Noah Webster entered Yale University in 1774. He interrupted his studies to serve in the American army during the Revolutionary War and then returned to school and graduated in 1778. After college, he became a teacher. He grew dissatisfied with the textbooks available for his students, so he wrote his own. In 1783, he published *The American Spelling Book*, which is perhaps the most famous spelling book ever created in the United States. Also known as "The Blue-Backed Speller" because it originally had a blue cover, the book has sold more than 100 million copies since it was published.

By the early 1800s, Webster decided that the country needed its own dictionary. In 1806 he published *A Compendious Dictionary of the English Language*, the first truly American dictionary. It was a small book by today's standards, but it was an important first step in a much larger project.

After finishing the *Compendious Dictionary*, Webster started work on the book that would be his masterpiece. He called it *An American Dictionary of the English Language*. It took more than 20 years to finish. When it was published in 1828, it set new standards for how dictionaries should be made. It had 70,000 entries, and it was the largest English dictionary ever published up to that time.

Webster introduced many new improvements in his dictionary. He was the first to include distinctively American words such as *skunk, hickory,* and *chowder*. He thought that many spelling rules were confusing, so he urged people to simplify the spelling of many words. For instance, he played an important part in convincing Americans to change the spelling of *musick* to *music, centre* to *center*, and *plough* to *plow*..

After a brilliant and distinguished career as a scholar, writer, and teacher, Noah Webster died in 1843 in Connecticut.

Twelve years earlier, in 1831, two brothers, George and Charles Merriam, opened a printing and bookselling company called the G. & C. Merriam Co. in Springfield, Massachusetts. (It was later renamed Merriam-Webster Inc.) After Webster's death, the brothers made an agreement with Webster's family that gave them the rights to publish new editions of Webster's dictionary. The first new edition was published in 1847. It was the first Merriam-Webster dictionary, and it began a publishing tradition that has continued uninterrupted to this day.

© 2004 Merriam-Webster Inc.

Words in Action

Imagine that you are a journalist and your editor has assigned you to interview Noah Webster. What questions would you ask him? Write a paragraph about what your interview would be like.

Web Field Trip

What was life like in Noah Webster's Day? Find out more about Mr. Webster's life and work by visiting the Web site of the Noah Webster House and Museum at http://noahwebsterhouse.org.

How to Use Your Dictionary

Alphabetical Order—Getting Started

auk

Your name _____

Scan your eyes down the columns on your dictionary page and you'll see that each of the **dictionary entries** begins with a **boldface** word that sticks out into the margin just a little to catch the eye. This boldface word is called the **entry word** or **main entry**.

> **aback** \ə-'bak\ *adv* : by surprise ⟨taken *aback* by the change in plan⟩
> **aba·cus** \'ab-ə-kəs\ *n, pl* **aba·ci** \'ab-ə-ˌsī\ *or* **aba·cus·es** : an instrument for doing arithmetic by sliding counters along rods or in grooves
> **abaft** \ə-'baft\ *adv* : toward or at the back part of a ship

One of the most important things to understand about a dictionary is that the main entries are arranged in **alphabetical order**. We call this **alphabetization**. To use a dictionary effectively, you'll need to become very familiar with alphabetization. It can take some practice, but once you get good at it, you'll be able to locate the words you are looking for with ease.

The basic concept of alphabetical order is simple. Since *a* comes before *b* and *b* comes before *c* in the alphabet, all of the words beginning with *a* come before those that begin with *b*, the *b* words come before the *c* words, and so on all the way through the dictionary.

> **ab·sence** \'ab-səns\ *n* **1** : a being away...
> **bank·er** \'bang-kər\ *n* : a person who...
> **cal·li·ope** \kə-'lī-ə-pē\ *n* : a keyboard...
> **de·light·ful** \di-'līt-fəl\ *adj* : giving delight...

est Your Alphabet Skills
Put each series of words in the correct alphabetical order.

1. cat, mouse, dog, horse, pig

_____ _____ _____ _____ _____

2. sled, jaunt, lyric, umbrella, TV

_____ _____ _____ _____ _____

3. vitamin, acrobat, lazy, octopus, noodle

_____ _____ _____ _____ _____

© 2004 Merriam-Webster Inc.

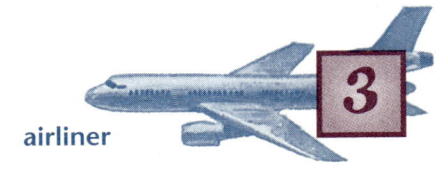

airliner

Your name _____

Alphabetical order also applies within each group of words that share the same first letter. This means that all of the words with the same first letter are then sorted by their second letter.

> **ear·ring** \ˈir-ˌring\ *n* : an ornament worn…
> **ed·i·ble** \ˈed-ə-bəl\ *adj* : fit or safe to eat
> **enig·ma** \i-ˈnig-mə\ *n* : something hard…

est Your Alphabet Skills
Put each series of words in the correct alphabetical order.

1. bad, broccoli, bike, boy, blouse

   _____ _____ _____ _____ _____

2. sunny, share, seven, snap, store

   _____ _____ _____ _____ _____

3. ivy, industry, ignition, icy, irk

   _____ _____ _____ _____ _____

Those words with the same first and second letters are then sorted according to their third letter. Words with the same first, second, and third letter are sorted according to their fourth letter, and so on.

> **fig** \ˈfig\ *n* : an edible fruit that is oblong…
> **fire·plug** \ˈfīr-ˌpləg\ *n* : HYDRANT
> **first·hand** \ˈfərst-ˈhand\ *adj or adv*…

est Your Alphabet Skills
Put each series of words in the correct alphabetical order.

1. chop, chalk, chili, cheese, chute

   _____ _____ _____ _____ _____

2. cannon, capstan, capacious, canopy, capable

   _____ _____ _____ _____ _____

3. dragonfly, dragnet, dragoon, draggle, dragon

   _____ _____ _____ _____ _____

4

© 2004 Merriam-Webster Inc.

Alphabetical Order—Moving Along

bulldozer

Your name _____

When words are arranged in alphabetical order, hyphens or spaces in the words don't count. You'll also want to ignore the **boldface** dots in the entry words when you are looking up words in the dictionary. (We'll explain what these dots are in lesson 4.) When you are trying to decide where a word with a hyphen, space, or boldface dot belongs in an alphabetized list, skip over that place in the word and look to the next letter.

Also, a word like **to** that has no letters after the second spot comes before a word like **toad**, with an **a** in the third spot. The entry **ill** comes before **illegal**, and so on.

> ³**high** *n* **1** : the space overhead : SKY ⟨watched the birds on *high*⟩ **2** : a region of high barometric pressure **3** : a high point or level ⟨prices reached a new *high*⟩ **4** : the arrangement of gears in an automobile giving the highest speed of travel
> **high·brow** \ˈhī-ˌbrau̇\ *n* : a person of great learning or culture
> **high fidelity** *n* : the reproduction of sound with a high degree of accuracy
> **long–lived** \ˈlȯng-ˈlīvd, -ˈlivd\ *adj* : living or lasting for a long time
> **long–range** \ˈlȯng-ˈrānj\ *adj* **1** : capable of traveling or shooting great distances **2** : lasting over or providing for a long period
> **long·sight·ed** \ˈlȯng-ˈsīt-əd\ *adj* : FARSIGHTED — **long·sight·ed·ness** *n*

Test Your Alphabet Skills
Put each series of dictionary entries in the correct alphabetical order.

1. fir, fire escape, fire·crack·er, figure out, figure of speech

    _____ _____ _____ _____ _____

2. al·lude, any·wise, any, any·one, all-star

    _____ _____ _____ _____ _____

3. double play, dou·ble, double bass, dou·ble·head·er, dou·ble·joint·ed

    _____ _____ _____ _____ _____

4. man·i·fold, man, man-made, man·age·ment, man·age

    _____ _____ _____ _____ _____

© 2004 Merriam-Webster Inc.

Your name _____

Alphabet Investigator

Zookeeper Alexis has called Detective Daniels to report trouble at the zoo. But the messages from headquarters got scrambled on the way to the detective's car.

Unscramble the messages so Detective Daniels can find out what is going on and get the investigation started.

Each box below contains words that are one part of the message Detective Daniels received. Write the words from each box on the lines at the right in alphabetical order to reveal the detective's assignment. Include proper names in alphabetical order too. Some message parts may include more than one sentence.

First part of message:

dromedaries	Alexis
foxes	ibexes
vanished	alligators
alleges	jackals
mysteriously	hedgehogs
elephants	

_____ _____ _____,
_____, _____,
_____ _____ _____,
_____, _____, _____.

Second part of message:

keepers	to
Concerned	Tower
Toucan	Report
panic	near

_____ _____
_____ _____.
_____ _____
_____ _____.

Third part of message:

zipper	yellow
white	suspect
investigate	with
wearing	windbreaker

_____ _____ _____
_____ _____ _____
_____ _____.

Words in Action

What do you think happens next in the Menagerie Mystery? How do you think Detective Daniels solves the case? Make up your own ending for the mystery. Write a story telling what Detective Daniels discovers at the zoo and how the mystery is solved.

© 2004 Merriam-Webster Inc.

3 Guide Words

Your name _____

If you've learned alphabetization, you've already mastered the most important skill you need to find the words you are looking for in the dictionary. But the dictionary also has a special feature that can help you find words even faster. To save you from having to search up and down page after page looking for the word you want, most dictionaries print a pair of **guide words** at the top of each page. They are usually the alphabetically first and last entry on the page. By looking at the guide words and thinking about whether the word you are hunting for will fit alphabetically between them, you can quickly move from page to page to find the right one.

Say, for example, you are looking up **thoughtful** and you have already turned to the section of words that begin with the letter **T**. You next should look at the guide words at the top of the pages. The exact guide words will vary from dictionary to dictionary, but you might, for example, see a page that has **thermostat · this** in its top corner, followed by a page with **thistle · thread**.

You know that **thoughtful** is alphabetically after **this**, the last guide word on the first page, so you want to look beyond that page. On the next page, you see the guide words **thistle** and **thread**. You know that **thoughtful** comes after **thistle** and before **thread**, so this must be the page you want.

thistle to thread

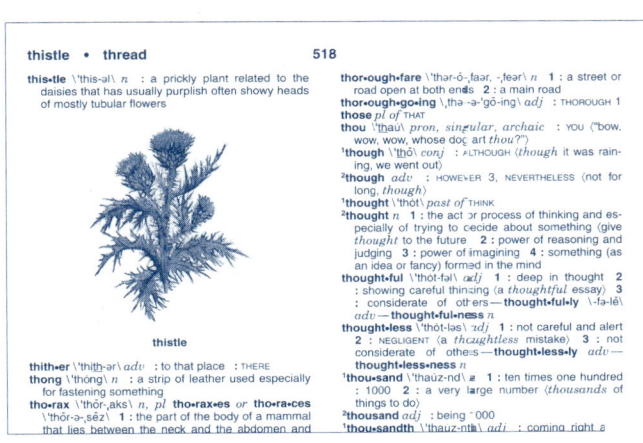

© 2004 Merriam-Webster Inc.

Your name _____

Test Your Guide Word Skills
Use the guide words to find the following words in your dictionary. Write the guide words in the spaces provided below.

1. counterfeit _____ _____
2. sculpture _____ _____
3. offshore _____ _____
4. messy _____ _____
5. however _____ _____
6. tangible _____ _____
7. babble _____ _____
8. gap _____ _____
9. colt _____ _____
10. collarbone _____ _____
11. siesta _____ _____
12. periscope _____ _____
13. saga _____ _____
14. barnyard _____ _____
15. banquet _____ _____
16. usable _____ _____
17. humorous _____ _____
18. hurtle _____ _____
19. adobe _____ _____
20. depth _____ _____

© 2004 Merriam-Webster Inc.

4 End-of-Line Divisions

daisy

Your name _____

Most of the entry words in the dictionary are shown with dots at several places in the word. These dots are not part of the spelling of the word. They are only there to show **end-of-line division**—places where you can put a hyphen if you have to break a word into two pieces because there is not room for all of it at the end of a line.

Let's say you are writing a story for school and you have come to the end of the line on your page. You have started to write the word *hippopotamus* when you realize you don't have enough space left for the whole word. You can write part of the word on one line, ending with a hyphen, and put the rest of it on the following line. But you shouldn't just break the word anywhere. There's a right way and a wrong way to do it—and you can find the right way at the word's entry in the dictionary.

> **hip·po·pot·a·mus** \,hip-ə-'pät-ə-məs\ *n*, *pl* **hip·po·pot·a·mus·es** *or* **hip·po·pot·a·mi** \-,mī\ : a large hoglike animal with thick hairless skin that eats plants and lives in African rivers

hippopotamus

In this example, the dots show four different places where you can break the word *hippopotamus* and put a hyphen.

hip-	popotamus
hippo-	potamus
hippopot-	amus
hippopota-	mus

Words should not be divided so that only one letter stays at the end of a line or comes at the beginning of the next line. This is the reason no dot is shown after the first letter of the word *abandon* or before the last letter of the word *banana*.

> ¹**aban·don** \ə-'ban-dən\ *vb*...
> **ba·nana** \bə-'nan-ə\ *n*...

When two or more main entries have the same spelling and the same end-of-line divisions, the dots indicating these divisions are shown only in the first of the entries.

> ¹**mo·tion** \'mō-shən\ *n*...
> ²**motion** *vb*...

You would divide the verb *motion* the same as the noun *motion*, but the dictionary shows the dots only once.

dragonfly

© 2004 Merriam-Webster Inc.

Your name _____

 egmenting Words

In the words below, put a dot at each place where the word can be divided at the end of a line. Use the dictionary to be sure you place the dots in the right spots.

1. emperor
2. snowman
3. crayon
4. oxygen
5. pizza
6. misconduct
7. pajamas
8. asteroid
9. teddy bear
10. macaw
11. teacher
12. global
13. zodiac
14. impersonal

15. pyramid
16. pickerel
17. platypus
18. obelisk
19. brother
20. relationship
21. education
22. pomegranate
23. importance
24. royalty
25. oriole
26. orangutan
27. octagon
28. tournament

 ords in Action

Newspaper reporters must use hyphens often to fit stories into small spaces. Write a news story about something that has happened to you. The story must fit in a space that is 3 inches tall and 2 inches wide. Use hyphens to segment at least three words in your story. Remember to include a headline!

© 2004 Merriam-Webster Inc.

5 Pronunciation

eggplant

Your name _____

One thing you will certainly notice as you look at your dictionary page is the strange-looking symbols that appear between slanted lines.

\ˈärd-ˌvärk\ \ˈdēp-ˈfrī\ \ˈhət\ \ˈtər-ˌmȯil\

These are the **pronunciation symbols**.

Dictionaries use pronunciation symbols to help you learn how each word should sound. In most cases, you'll see a respelling of the word using pronunciation symbols directly after the **boldface** entry word.

> **sauce** \ˈsȯs\ *n* **1** : a tasty liquid poured over food **2** : stewed fruit ⟨cranberry *sauce*⟩
> **sauce·pan** \ˈsȯs-ˌpan\ *n* : a small deep cooking pan with a handle
> **sau·cer** \ˈsȯ-sər\ *n* : a small shallow dish often with a slightly lower center for holding a cup

Each pronunciation symbol stands for one important sound in English. To help you "decode" each sound, your dictionary has included special **pronunciation keys**. In the keys, the symbols are followed by words that contain the sound of each symbol.

ā... d**a**y, f**a**de, m**a**te, v**a**cation

The boldface letters in the words in the key below show by example the sounds that the symbols represent. In other words, the key tells you that whenever you see the symbol **a**, you should pronounce it the way you would pronounce the boldface vowel sounds in the words *day, fade, mate,* and *vacation.*

You'll find a large key at the beginning of the dictionary showing all of the symbols, and you'll find a smaller key showing some of the symbols at the bottom of the odd-numbered pages of the book.

\ə\ ab**u**t	\au̇\ **ou**t	\i\ t**i**p	\ȯ\ s**aw**
\u̇\ f**oo**t	\ər\ f**ur**ther	\ch\ **ch**in	
\ī\ l**i**fe	\ȯi\ c**oi**n	\y\ **y**et	\a\ m**a**t
\e\ p**e**t	\j\ **j**ob	\th\ **th**in	\yü\ f**ew**
\ā\ t**a**ke	\ē\ **ea**sy	\ng\ si**ng**	\th̲\ **th**is
\yu̇\ c**u**re	\ä\ c**o**t, c**a**rt	\g\ **g**o	
\ō\ b**o**ne	\ü\ f**oo**d	\zh\ vi**si**on	

Until you've learned the sound for each symbol, you should refer to the keys often as you sound out pronunciations in the dictionary.

ermine

© 2004 Merriam-Webster Inc.

Your name _____

hat's That Sound?

Here are eight sets of pronunciations for eight words. For each word, there are three possibilities. Using the dictionary, find the correct pronunciation for each word and put a check next to it.

   Note: We'll explain about the hyphens and the stress marks (which look like this ' or this ˌ) in the next lesson. You can ignore them for now.

1. hunch	___'hench	___'hunch	___'hənch
2. ecology	___u-'kal-a-jē	___i-'käl-ə-jē	___e-'kol-i-je
3. percussion	___pər-'kəsh-ən	___par-'kich-in	___por-'kich-ən
4. shamrock	___'shäm-ˌrok	___'sham-ˌrək	___'sham-ˌräk
5. zodiac	___'zod-e-ˌak	___'zōd-ē-ˌak	___'zud-e-ˌak
6. hibernate	___'hī-bər-ˌnāt	___'hi-ber-ˌnat	___'hə-bər-ˌnät
7. fiesta	___fi-'es-'tē	___fa-'es-te	___fē-'es-tə
8. useful	___'üs-ful	___'yus-fül	___'yüs-fəl

hat's That Word?

Use the pronunciation keys in your dictionary to "decode" the pronunciations on the left. Draw a line connecting each pronunciation to the correct word on the right.

1. hot dog	\\'ap-əl\\
2. fun	\\im-ˌaj-ə-'nā-shən\\
3. onion	\\'hōm-ˌwərk\\
4. imagination	\\'fan\\
5. fine	\\'ən-yən\\
6. apple	\\'fin\\
7. south	\\'jī-ənt\\
8. fin	\\'hät-ˌdȯg\\
9. homework	\\'fən\\
10. fan	\\'saůth\\
11. giant	\\'fīn\\

© 2004 Merriam-Webster Inc.

More About Pronunciation

Your name _____

feather

Many of the pronunciations in the dictionary are broken into smaller sections, called **syllables**. Merriam-Webster dictionaries use hyphens with the pronunciation symbols to show the syllables of a word, as in these examples.

> **flea** \'flē\ *n*...
>   (1 syllable)
> **bed·side** \'bed-ˌsīd\ *n*...
>   (2 syllables)
> **east·er·ly** \'ē-stər-lē\ *adj* or *adv*...
>   (3 syllables)
> **op·ti·mism** \'äp-tə-ˌmiz-əm\ *n*...
>   (4 syllables)

Some syllables of a word are spoken with greater force, or **stress**, than others. Three kinds of stress are shown in Merriam-Webster dictionaries.

Primary stress, or **strong stress**, is shown by a high mark (like this ') placed before a syllable. The first syllable of **easterly** has a primary stress in our example. This means it gets spoken with a little extra force when you say the word. To see what we mean, try saying the word *easterly* several times out loud putting the stress on a different syllable each time. It should sound a little strange to you when you put the emphasis on the second or third syllables.

Secondary stress, or **medium stress**, is shown by a low mark (like this ˌ) before a syllable. The second syllable in **bedside** and the third syllable in **optimism** have secondary stress. Secondary stress means the syllable is spoken with some force, but not as much as with primary stress.

The third kind of stress, **weak stress**, has no mark before syllables. These syllables are the ones that are spoken without much force at all.

Each of the three kinds of stress is shown in the pronunciation of **penmanship**.

> **pen·man·ship** \'pen-mən-ˌship\ *n*...

The first syllable has primary stress. The second syllable has weak stress. The third syllable has secondary stress. Say the word to yourself so you can hear each kind of stress.

flea

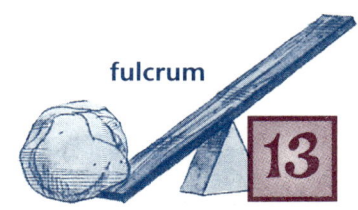
fulcrum

© 2004 Merriam-Webster Inc.

Your name _____

Find the Syllables

Look up the following words in your dictionary. Insert the missing hyphens in the correct spot of each pronunciation.

favorable \ˈf ā v ə r ə b ə l\

dinosaur \ˈd ī n ə ˌs ȯ r\

runaway \ˈr ə n ə ˌw ā\

outpatient \ˈa u̇ t ˌp ā s h ə n t\

papaya \p ə ˈp ī ə\

recorder \r i ˈk ȯ r d ə r\

apologize \ə ˈp ä l ə ˌj ī z\

majesty \ˈm a j ə s t ē\

pacific \p ə ˈs i f i k\

television \ˈt e l ə ˌv i z h ə n\

All Stressed Out

Here are some pronunciations that are missing their stress marks. Look up the words, then write in **primary** and **secondary stress** for each pronunciation.

holiday \ häl- ə- dā\

magpie \ mag- pī\

toothbrush \ tüth- brəsh\

topsy-turvy \ täp- sē- tər- vē\

katydid \ kāt- ē- did\

foolhardy \ fül- härd- ē\

probability \ präb- ə- bil- ət- ē\

sedimentary \ sed- ə- ment- ə- rē\

wayside \ wā- sīd\

navigation \ nav- ə- gā- shən\

Putting It All Together

Look up the following words. Add the hyphens *and* the stress marks to the pronunciations.

navy \ n ā v ē\

teenager \ t ē n ā j ə r\

telepathy \ t ə l e p ə t h ē\

alumna \ ə l ə m n ə\

meteor \ m ē t ē ə r\

strawberry \ s t r ȯ b e r ē\

everyday \ e v r ē d ā\

luminous \ l ü m ə n ə s\

zodiac \ z ō d ē a k\

finale \ f ə n a l ē\

14

7 Still More About Pronunciation

gibbon

Your name _____

Many words are pronounced in more than one way. Two or more pronunciations for a single entry are separated by commas, as in this example.

¹ra·tion \'rash-ən, 'rā-shən\ n...

The order in which different pronunciations for the same word are given does not mean that the pronunciation given first is somehow better or more correct than the others. Both pronunciations of **ration** are equally acceptable, for example. You can choose the pronunciation that sounds most natural to you—you will be correct whichever one you use.

Sometimes when a second or third pronunciation is shown, only part of the pronunciation of the word changes. When this happens, the dictionary may show only the section that changes.

greasy \'grē-sē, -zē\ adj...
pa·ja·mas \pə-'jäm-əz, -'jam-əz\ n pl...

To get the full second or third pronunciation of a word, add the part that changes to the part that does not change. The second pronunciation of **greasy** is \'grē-zē\ and the second pronunciation of **pajamas** is \pə-'jam-əz\.

If two or more entries are spelled the same and have the same pronunciation, your dictionary will show the pronunciation of only the first of these entries.

¹se·cure \si-'kyu̇r\ adj...
²secure vb...

Because these two words are pronounced alike, they are called **homophones**. Because they are also spelled alike, they are also called **homographs**. In lesson 10, you'll learn more about homographs.

Many compound entries are made up of two or three separate words. If the dictionary does not show a pronunciation for all or part of such an entry, the missing pronunciation is the same as that for the individual word or words as given at their own entries.

milk shake n : a drink made of milk, a flavoring syrup, and ice cream shaken or mixed thoroughly
¹**milk** \'milk\ n...
¹**shake** \'shāk\ vb...

No pronunciation is shown for the entry **milk shake**. This means that the two words are pronounced just like the separate entries **milk** and **shake**.

Some dictionary entries have additional boldface words just after the entry word or at the end of the entry. (In upcoming lessons, we'll discuss why this happens.) In such cases, the dictionary may show only part of the pronunciation.

grasshopper

© 2004 Merriam-Webster Inc.

15

Your name _____

> **post·pone** \pōst-ˈpōn\ *vb*... —
> **post·pone·ment** \-mənt\ *n*
> **sub·head** \ˈsəb-ˌhed\ or **sub·head·ing**
> \-ˌhed-ing\ *n*

This means that the rest of the word is pronounced the same as part of the main entry. The pronunciation of **postponement** is \pōst-ˈpōn-mənt\. **Subheading** is pronounced \ˈsəb-ˌhed-ing\.

Sometimes a boldface word at the end of an entry will show no pronunciation at all. In these cases the pronunciation of the word is the same as the pronunciation of the main entry plus the pronunciation of a special word ending called a **suffix**. The pronunciation of the suffix is found at its own alphabetical place in the dictionary.

> **rusty** \ˈrəs-tē\ *adj*... — **rust·i·ness** *n*
> **-ness** \nəs\ *n suffix*...

In the example above, the entry **rustiness** is pronounced \ˈrəs-tē-nəs\.

e a Dictionary Detective

Use your dictionary to write the correct pronunciations for each term. You might have to check more than one entry or combine pronunciations from two entries.

nerve fiber _____

²exhaust *n* _____

extinguisher _____

storminess _____

conclusively _____

managership _____

eyeteeth _____

outboard motor _____

faithfully _____

pled _____

ords in Action

The Contrary cousins always disagree. Today, they are arguing about the word *economic*. They say it differently, but each cousin insists his pronunciation is the correct one. Check the pronunciation of *economic* in the dictionary. Then write the conversation between the Contrary cousins. Tell which pronunciation each one uses and why both cousins are right.

16

© 2004 Merriam-Webster Inc.

Variants

hemlock

Your name _____

Some words have more than one correct spelling. In such cases, you may see a second or third spelling, also in boldface type, after the main entry word in the dictionary. These additional spellings are called **variant spellings** or simply **variants**.

scep·ter *or* **scep·tre** \'sep-tər\ *n* : a rod carried by a ruler as a sign of authority

This entry tells us that **scepter** and **sceptre** are both accepted as correct spellings of the word.

Variant or Misspelling?

Each of the following pairs contains an entry word followed by a second spelling that may or may not be an accepted variant. Use your dictionary to find out if the second spelling is okay or not. Cross out any unacceptable spellings.

1.	**capital**	capitle		13.	**sulfur**	sulphur
2.	**barnacle**	barnickle		14.	**rhyme**	ryme
3.	**caliph**	calif		15.	**rigorous**	riggorous
4.	**caliper**	calipper		16.	**backward**	backwards
5.	**bogey**	bogie		17.	**syrup**	sirrup
6.	**ballast**	ballust		18.	**bluing**	blueing
7.	**garage**	garaje		19.	**fjord**	fiord
8.	**pom-pom**	pompon		20.	**incentive**	insentive
9.	**poinsettia**	poinsetta		21.	**fuse**	fuze
10	**peddler**	peddlar		22.	**mold**	mould
11.	**synapse**	sinapse		23.	**bark**	barque
12.	**salable**	saleable		24.	**barrel**	barel

helicopter

© 2004 Merriam-Webster Inc.

Your name _____

All of the variants shown in the dictionary are correct, but some are used more often in writing than others. When you see two variants separated by *or*, you can assume that both forms are common. Usually they will simply be listed in alphabetical order, like **scepter** *or* **sceptre**.

If one form is slightly more common than the other, however, it will be listed first, even if that means the variants will be out of alphabetical order.

Gyp·sy *or* **Gip·sy** \\'jip-sē\ *n*...

In the previous example, the order of the variants tells you that **Gypsy** is used more often than **Gipsy**.

Sometimes you will also see a variant spelling shown after the word *also*.

pea \\'pē\ *n, pl* **peas** *also* **pease** \\'pēz\...

The *also* tells you that the next spelling is much less common than the first, although it is still a correct spelling.

Which Is Preferred?

Here are some words that have more than one spelling. The possibilities for each word are given in alphabetical order. One of the two choices given is preferred over the other. Circle the preferred spelling for each word—and pay careful attention! In several cases alternate forms exist for the plural or another form of the word. In these cases, the main entry is given in parentheses.

hoofs, hooves (hoof)

judgement, judgment

smelled, smelt (smell)

fungi, funguses (fungus)

shod, shoed (shoe)

ox, oxen (ox)

vacua, vacuums (vacuum)

quartet, quartette

juncoes, juncos (junco)

eerie, eery

encrust, incrust

shrank, shrunk (shrink)

hooray, hurrah

hooray, hurray

hurrah, hurray

distil, distill

among, amongst

biceps, bicepses (biceps)

9 Functional Labels

iceberg

Your name _____

Frisky puppies happily romp and frolic.
(adjective) (noun) (adverb) (verb) (conjunction) (verb)

Words are used in many different ways in a sentence. For example, if a word is used for the name of something **(car, house, rainbow)** it is called a **noun**. If it describes an action or a state of being **(run, stand, live, is)** the word is a **verb**. Words that show a quality of something **(tall, sleepy, fast)** are **adjectives**, and words that tell how, when, or where something happens **(quickly, very, yesterday, here)** are **adverbs**. **Pronouns (them, you, that)** are words which substitute for nouns, and **conjunctions (and, but, yet)** join two words or groups of words. **Prepositions (to, for, by)** combine with nouns and pronouns to form phrases that answer such questions as where?, how?, and which?, and **interjections (hi, adios, ouch)** stand alone and often show a feeling or a reaction to something rather than a meaning.

To show you how the various entry words are used, or how they function in a sentence, dictionaries use **functional labels** before the definitions. In Merriam-Webster dictionaries, these labels are usually abbreviations in slanting *italic* type, and they come right after the pronunciation—when one is shown—or immediately after the entry word.

sea·coast \ˈsē-ˌkōst\ *n* : the shore of the sea
sitting room *n* : LIVING ROOM

The eight most common functions, known as parts of **parts of speech**, are shown in the examples below.

noun	²**cereal** *n*...
verb	**sing** \ˈsiŋ\ *vb*...
adjective	**hos·tile** \ˈhäst-l\ *adj*...
adverb	²**just** *adv*...
pronoun	¹**none** \ˈnən\ *pron*...
conjunction	²**since** *conj*...
preposition	²**under** *prep*...
interjection	⁴**why** \ˈwī, ˈhwī\ *interj*...

frisky puppies

ibex

Your name _____

Birds of a Feather

Each of the following words functions as one or more of the eight most common parts of speech. Write the words on the lines after the appropriate functional labels. Be careful—you'll have to write some words on more than one line, so check the dictionary carefully.

go	cloud	beside	these
anywhere	but	ouch	adorable
dictionary	by	strangely	because
because of	computer	well	she
between	hello	our	awful
or	remember	scorpion	oh
nor	you	succeed	into
brief	and	hey	run

vb _____

n _____

adj _____

adv _____

pron _____

conj _____

prep _____

interj _____

Words in Action

Are you good at word games? Here's one for you! Look at the words in the "Birds of a Feather" activity. See how many sentences you can make using only those words. If you need to, you can make nouns plural or change the verb tense to make your sentences make sense. Write down as many sentences as you can.

© 2004 Merriam-Webster Inc.

10 Homographs

jack-in-the-pulpit

Your name _____

Often you will find two, three, or more main entries that come one after another and are spelled exactly alike.

> ¹**seal** \'sēl\ *n* **1** : a sea mammal that swims with flippers, lives mostly in cold regions, mates and bears young on land, eats flesh, and is hunted for fur, hides, or oil **2** : the soft dense fur of a northern seal
> ²**seal** *n* **1** : something (as a pledge) that makes safe or secure **2** : a device with a cut or raised design or figure that can be stamped or pressed into wax or paper **3** : a piece of wax stamped with a design and used to seal a letter or package **4** : a stamp that may be used to close a letter or package ⟨Christmas *seals*⟩ **5** : something that closes tightly **6** : a closing that is tight and perfect
> ³**seal** *vb* **1** : to mark with a seal **2** : to close or make fast with or as if with a seal — **seal·er** *n*

Although these words look alike, they are different words because they come from different sources and so have different meanings, or because they are used in different ways in the sentence.

These similar entries are called **homographs** (from **homo-** "the same" and **-graph** "something written").

As we learned in lesson 7, these words are also called **homophones**, because they are pronounced alike.

Each homograph has a small raised number before it. This number is used in the dictionary entry to show that these are different words. The number is not used in writing the word.

Let's look closely at the homographs for **seal** to see just why they are different. The first entry, a noun, is defined as "a sea mammal." The second **seal** entry is also a noun, but its meanings are completely different from the meaning of the first entry. The third homograph of **seal** is certainly related to the second, but ³**seal** is a verb and, since it has a different use in the sentence, we show it as a different entry word.

¹seal

jellyfish

21

© 2004 Merriam-Webster Inc.

Your name _____

Which Is Which?
Look up the homographs in slanted italic text below and put the number of the correct entry on the line before the phrase.

____ tides *creep* up the beach

____ ghost stories give us the *creeps*

____ piles of *junk* in every corner

____ the flotilla of *junks* sailed into the harbor

____ they *junked* the old car

____ an angry *dispute* between neighbors

____ he *disputes* our version

____ a quick *peep* at the pile of presents

____ the quiet *peep* of the new chick

____ frogs *peep* noisily in the spring

Two for the Price of One
Choose the homograph below that can be used to fill in both blanks in the sentence. The word must make sense in both blanks. You can make nouns plural or change the tense of a verb to make the sentence make sense.

base   can   express   fall   fan   light   low   right   tense

1. In the _____ the leaves _____ to the ground.

2. The basketball _____ _____ themselves in the hot auditorium.

3. The _____ answer is _____ in front of you.

4. The _____ of the statue is made of _____ metal.

5. She felt her muscles _____ as the situation grew _____.

6. _____ you open this _____ for me?

7. Let's turn off the _____ and _____ a candle.

8. He _____ a desire to have the package sent by _____ mail.

9. The cow's _____ is a _____ sound.

Words in Action
Look up *bark* in the dictionary. It has quite a few homographs. Write an adventure story that uses all of the homographs of *bark*.

© 2004 Merriam-Webster Inc.

Inflected Forms

koala

Your name _____

You have probably noticed by now that some dictionary entries contain other **boldface** words in addition to the first one (the main entry). Some of these boldface words are called inflected forms. In Merriam-Webster dictionaries, the inflected forms usually come after the function label in the entry.

¹**echo** \\'ek-ō\ *n, pl* **ech·oes**…
²**guide** *vb* **guid·ed; guid·ing**…
hot \\'hät\ *adj* **hot·ter; hot·test**…

Inflected forms show the different forms that words can take depending on how they are being used. When we want to talk about more than one of something, English speakers use a special form of the noun called the **plural** form. **Echoes** is the plural form of **echo**. We also use special forms or **tenses** of verbs when we want to show that something has happened already (**guided**) or is happening now (**guiding**). And when we want to show how one thing is compared with another or with all others of the same kind, we use special forms of adjectives and adverbs called the **comparative** and **superlative** forms (**hotter** and **hottest**).

For most words, inflected forms are made in a regular way. Plurals are formed simply by adding *-s* or *-es* to the base word (one cat, two cat*s*; one box, two box*es*). Verb inflections are formed by adding *-ed* (yesterday I walk*ed* to school), *-ing* (I was walk*ing* down the street), and *-s* or *-es* (she walk*s* her dog; he wash*es* his car). Comparative and superlative forms are formed by adding *-er* and *-est*, or with the words *more* and *most* (a fast*er* computer; the high*est* mountain; a *more* natural appearance; the *most* ridiculous story).

Dictionaries do not usually show regular inflections.

bri·gade \bri-'gād\ *n* **1** : a body of soldiers consisting of two or more regiments…
dif·fer \\'dif-ər\ *vb* **1** : to be not the same : be unlike…

When you see entries like the examples **brigade**, and **differ**, you will know that the inflected forms are regular. *Brigade* becomes *brigades;* and *differ* becomes *differed, differing,* and *differs.*

Dictionaries often do show the inflections, however, when they are formed in any way other than by simply adding a regular ending or when we think someone might have a question about how they are formed, spelled or pronounced.

deer \\'dir\ *n, pl* **deer**…
go \\'gō\ *vb* **went** \\'went\; **gone** \\'gȯn\; **go·ing** \\'gō-ing\; **goes**…
prop·er·ty \\'präp-ərt-ē\ *n, pl* **prop·er·ties**…

kangaroo

Your name _____

nimals and Others

Here are 16 nouns that all form plurals in unusual ways. Some of them even have two plural forms. In the blank after each word write the plural form(s).

mantis	_____	knife	_____
fungus	_____	flamingo	_____
fez	_____	half	_____
dromedary	_____	quail	_____
trachea	_____	chassis	_____
reindeer	_____	goose	_____
fish	_____	hoof	_____
wolf	_____	octopus	_____

It Happened One Morning

Complete the paragraph below by filling in the blanks. Write the correct inflected forms of the verbs in parentheses.

Yesterday, I (wake) _____ up in the morning and (see) _____ a deer eating outside my window. I also (hear) _____ a bird singing. It (sing) _____ until a dog (come) _____ along and (scare) _____ it away. Then the dog (lie) _____ down in the sun and (take) _____ a nap.

Good, Better, Best

Some of these adjectives form comparative and superlative forms in the regular way, and some do not. Write the correct comparative and superlative forms on the lines provided.

1. good   *better   best*
2. bad   _____
3. green   _____
4. happy   _____
5. wry   _____
6. far   _____

7. zany   _____
8. windy   _____
9. fat   _____
10. small _____
11. narrow _____
12. muddy _____

© 2004 Merriam-Webster Inc.

12 Usage Labels

Your name _____

¹lever 1

In addition to functional labels, Merriam-Webster dictionaries use another kind of *italic* label to give information about how a word is used. **Usage labels** come after the functional labels or, if they apply only to a particular meaning, just before the beginning of the definition.

> **earth** \\'ərth\ *n* **1** : ²SOIL 1... **3** *often cap*
>   : the planet that we live on
> **french fry** *n, often cap 1st F* : a strip of
>   potato fried in deep fat...
> **ma** \\'mä, 'mȯ\ *n, often cap* : ¹MOTHER 1
> **no·el** \nō-'el\ *n* **1** : a Christmas carol
>   **2** *cap* : the Christmas season

One of the things the usage label may tell you is whether or not a particular word is sometimes written with a capital letter. Whenever a word is always or usually written with a capital letter, it has a capital letter in the main entry.

> **Thurs·day** \\'thərz-dē\ *n* : the fifth day
>   of the week

But some words are written with a small letter or a capital letter about equally often. These entries have an italic label *often cap*, like **ma** above. Other words are written with a capital letter in some meanings and not in others. These words are usually shown in the dictionary with a small first letter. The italic label tells you when the sense is always spelled with a capital letter (*cap*, like sense **2** of **noel**) or very frequently spelled with a capital letter (*often cap*, like sense **3** of **earth**). Can you tell what the usage label at the entry **french fry** means? If you would expect to see the word sometimes spelled *French fry* you're absolutely right.

Another thing the usage labels can tell you is whether a word or particular meaning is limited in use. One kind of word with limited use is a word that is not used much anymore although it was quite common a long time ago.

> **thou** \\'thau̇\ *pron, singular, archaic*
>   : YOU...

Thou is entered in the dictionary because you may sometimes see it in very old writings—in some versions of the Bible, for example.

The last kind of usage label tells you that a certain word or meaning is most commonly used in a limited area of the English-speaking world.

> ²**lift** *n* **1** : the amount that may be lifted
>   at one time : LOAD... **4** *chiefly British*
>   : ELEVATOR 2...

Here you see that meaning **4** is labeled *chiefly British*. This means that the word in this meaning is used more often in Great Britain than in the United States.

loggerhead

25

Your name _____

Getting It Right

Pick the correct choice to complete the sentence and write the letter in the blank.

1. The word *dalmatian* is _____.

    a) always capitalized   b) never capitalized   c) often capitalized

2. When the word *treasury* is capitalized, it refers to _____.

    a) a pirate's chest   b) a government department

    c) a place where money collected is kept and paid out

3. The adjective *bonny* is _____.

    a) often capitalized   b) archaic   c) used most often in Britain

4. The two most usual stylings of the verb *x-ray* are _____.

    a) x-ray and X-ray   b) x-Ray and X-Ray   c) X-Ray and X-ray

5. The pronoun *ye* is _____.

    a) often capitalized   b) archaic   c) used most often in Britain

6. The noun *thoroughbred* is capitalized when it means _____.

    a) a fine person   b) a purebred animal   c) a breed of racing horses

7. The word *mercury* is _____.

    a) always capitalized   b) capitalized in a specific use   c) never capitalized

8. The word *norman* is _____.

    a) sometimes capitalized   b) almost always capitalized   c) archaic

9. The word *soloist* is _____.

    a) British   b) usually capitalized   c) not usually capitalized

10. The label at *plaster of paris* is _____.

    a) *often cap 2d P*   b) *archaic*   c) *often cap 1st P*

11. The letters of the alphabet (*a, b, c,* etc.) are _____.

    a) often capitalized   b) capitalized in a specific use   c) never capitalized

12. The word *north* is sometimes capitalized when it is a(n) _____.

    a) adjective   b) adverb   c) noun

© 2004 Merriam-Webster Inc.

13 Definitions— Meaning

Your name _____

Definitions are what many people consider the most important part of the dictionary, because meanings are what people usually think of when they think of a dictionary.

Every definition in Merriam-Webster dictionaries starts with a **boldface** colon (:). The colon is used for each definition, even when there are two or more definitions for the same meaning.

---
in·trep·id \in-'trep-əd\ *adj* : feeling no fear : BOLD — **in·trep·id·ly** *adv*

The entry **intrepid**, for example, has two colons and two definitions. The definitions ("feeling no fear" and "bold") have the same basic meaning, but each is using different words to explain the same thing. (We'll explain why "bold" is in all capital letters in lesson 15.)

Many of the words entered in the dictionary have more than one meaning or **sense**, however. These separate meanings are shown by boldface numbers placed in front of the colons.

---
mill·er \'mil-ər\ *n* **1** : a person who works in or runs a flour mill **2** : a moth whose wings seem to be covered with flour or dust

---

There may be times when you will look up a word and be unsure which of several senses is the right one for the use you are checking. In such cases, you'll need to look closely at the definitions to see which is the best fit for the situation.

Suppose you are reading the sentence "A miller flies by and lands on a lampshade" and you are not certain what *miller* means. You look up the word in your dictionary and find two different meanings. How can you tell which is the right one? Take a look at the sentence again. Would it make sense for "a person who works in or runs a flour mill" to fly by and land on a lampshade? Probably not. But that certainly sounds like something "a moth whose wings seem to be covered with flour or dust" might do.

© 2004 Merriam-Webster Inc.

Your name _____

Look It Up

Look up each word and write the letter of the correct meaning in the blank.

1. baste _____
    a) a starting place or goal in various games   b) to moisten while roasting
    c) to lie or relax in pleasantly warm surroundings   d) to hit very hard

2. dell _____
    a) to dig deeply into the earth   b) a small valley   c) an indefinite amount
    d) lacking brightness or luster

3. frazzle _____
    a) a tired or nervous condition   b) filled with fear   c) not controlled by others
    d) recently hatched or very young fishes

4. mart _____
    a) to set apart by a line or boundary   b) gloom, darkness
    c) the state of being merry or happy as shown by laughter   d) a trading place

Context Is Key

Which definition best fits the italic word in the phrases below? Write the letter in the blank.

1. reading the ancient *classics* _____
    a) a written work or author of ancient Greece or Rome
    b) a great work of art   c) something outstanding of its kind

2. *scored* the wood with a knife _____
    a) to set down in an account   b) to keep the score in a game
    c) to cut or mark with a line, scratch, or notch

3. legally *bound* to report the incident _____
    a) tied or fastened with or as if with bands   b) required by law or duty
    c) covered with binding

© 2004 Merriam-Webster Inc.

14 Definitions— Historical Order

Your name _____

How do dictionary editors decide which meaning to list first? In Merriam-Webster dictionaries, the order is **historical**, which means it reflects the order in which the different meanings came into use.

> **skim** \\'skim\\ *vb* **skimmed; skim·ming**
> **1** : to clean a liquid of scum or floating substance : remove (as cream or film) from the top part of a liquid **2** : to read or examine quickly and not thoroughly **3** : to throw so as to skip along the surface of water **4** : to pass swiftly or lightly over

Let's look at meaning number **1** of **skim**. This meaning first came into use in English many centuries ago, and through the years it gained a more specific use, that of taking the cream off milk. This specific use is shown as the second definition at meaning **1**. The second definition does not change the original meaning; it only adds a little.

Meaning **2** of **skim** seems to have come into use as a figure of speech. If you think of a spoon barely touching the surface of water or milk or going just under the surface to scoop off something, you realize that the scoop is only taking off what can be seen on the surface. Most of the liquid remains behind. By first applying the word *skim* to reading or examining something and only getting what could be seen "on the surface" without going more deeply into the work, someone was using *skim* as a figure of speech. As more and more people used the word in this way, it came to have a set meaning.

Meaning **3**, which developed after meanings **1** and **2**, seems to have come from the first meaning in a similar way. This time, though, the idea of "just touching" a surface was the one that carried over to the act of causing rocks or other objects to bounce along the surface of a body of water.

Can you guess how meaning **4** came into use? Here it seems the meaning moved one more step away, from the idea of "just touching the surface" to that of "just missing the surface."

With the entry **skim**, you can see just how the word grew from one meaning to four. And the arrangement of the four meanings in historical order lets you follow that growth.

© 2004 Merriam-Webster Inc.

Your name _____

Tried and True
Which meaning is the oldest? Write the answer in the blank.

1. bowl _____
    a) to hit with or as if with something rolled   b) to move rapidly and smoothly as rolling   c) to roll a ball in bowling

2. crust _____
    a) the hardened outside surface of bread   b) the pastry cover of a pie   c) the outer part of the earth's surface

3. gentility _____
    a) the qualities of a well-bred person   b) good manners   c) good birth and family

4. reserve _____
    a) caution in one's words and behavior   b) something stored or available for future use   c) an area of land set apart

Cutting Edge
Which meaning is the most recent? Write the answer in the blank.

1. apt _____
    a) quick to learn   b) having a tendency   c) just right

2. kink _____
    a) cramp   b) a short tight twist or curl   c) an imperfection that makes something hard to use or work

3. plain _____
    a) clear to the mind   b) not handsome or beautiful   c) having no pattern or decoration

4. raw ____
    a) not trained or experienced   b) not cooked   c) unpleasantly damp or cold

Words in Action
Is a house always a home? Look up the noun *house* in the dictionary. Create a chart or graph showing how the meaning of *house* has changed over time. Show which meanings came first, which came next, and which developed most recently. Tell how you know.

© 2004 Merriam-Webster Inc.

15 Synonyms and Cross-references

octopus

Your name _____

In Merriam-Webster dictionaries, you will often see words in definitions that are printed entirely in SMALL CAPITAL letters. Any word in small capital letters following a boldface colon is a **synonym** of the entry word. This is to say, it has the same or nearly the same meaning as the entry word.

per·haps \pər-'haps\ *adv* : possibly but not certainly : MAYBE

We see the synonym MAYBE in the entry **perhaps**, for example. *Maybe* is a word that also means "possibly but not certainly," just as *perhaps* does.

Sometimes an entry is defined only by a synonym.

mail carrier *n* : LETTER CARRIER

In the entry **mail carrier**, LETTER CARRIER is a **cross-reference** referring you to the entry **letter carrier**. There you will find a definition that also applies to **mail carrier**.

letter carrier *n* : a person who delivers mail

You now know that the word *mail carrier* means "a person who delivers mail." Cross-references save space in dictionaries because they take up less room than printing the full definition in two places.

Sometimes you will see a number used as part of the cross-reference, as at the entry **feign**.

feign \'fān\ *vb* : PRETEND 2

The cross-reference to PRETEND 2 tells you that the definition found at sense 2 of **pretend** also fits **feign**.

pre·tend \pri-'tend\ *vb* **1** : to make believe : SHAM **2** : to put forward as true something that is not true ⟨*pretend* friendship⟩ — **pre·tend·er** *n*

The entry word and the synonym will always have the same part of speech. Thus, if the synonym of a verb is an entry with two or more homographs, you will always know that the right entry will be the homograph that is a verb. Nevertheless, your dictionary helps you by showing the proper homograph number at the cross-reference when necessary.

prick·er \'prik-ər\ *n* : ¹PRICKLE 1

In the entry **pricker**, the cross-reference is telling you to look at meaning 1 of the first homograph of **prickle**.

¹prick·le \'prik-əl\ *n* **1** : a small sharp point (as a thorn) **2** : a slight stinging pain

overhand knot

© 2004 Merriam-Webster Inc.

Your name _____

Synonyms, Synonyms

Use your dictionary to find the synonyms for the words given here.
Write the synonyms on the lines next to the words.

1. engender _____
2. hallway _____
3. bring about _____
4. predicament _____
5. thickset _____
6. insignificant _____

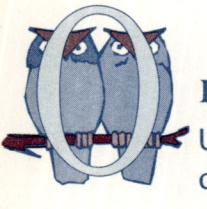

7. habitual _____
8. malt _____
9. inwardly _____
10. shimmer _____
11. inkling _____
12. mote _____

One Step, Two Step

Use your dictionary and your cross-reference skills to identify the correct definition for the following words. Write the letter in the blank.

1. beau _____
   a) a regular male companion of a girl or woman   b) a beautiful girl or woman
   c) a candy with a soft coating and a creamy center

2. cinder _____
   a) a North American tree that has needles and small egg-shaped cones
   b) a red mineral consisting of a sulfide of mercury
   c) the waste left after the melting of ores and the separation of metal from them

3. hoarfrost _____
   a) to cover with frost or with something suggesting frost
   b) temperature cold enough to cause freezing   c) a covering of tiny ice crystals

4. incline _____
   a) upward or downward slant   b) a piece of slanting ground
   c) a turn for the worse

5. norm _____
   a) to amount to usually   b) something usual in a group, class, or series
   c) being ordinary or usual

© 2004 Merriam-Webster Inc.

Verbal Illustrations

parrot

Your name _____

At times you may look up a word in your dictionary and understand the definition but still be unsure about the right way to use the word. Sometimes a word has several similar meanings and can be used in a sentence in different ways.

To help you understand the more difficult words and usages, Merriam-Webster dictionaries include brief phrases or sentences called **verbal illustrations** following many definitions. A verbal illustration shows you a typical use of the word. It comes after the definition and is enclosed in angle brackets, like this ⟨ ⟩. The entry word, or an inflected form of it, appears in the verbal illustration in italic type.

At the entry **snap**, for example, most of the definitions have verbal illustrations to show how the word is used in each meaning.

> ¹**snap** \'snap\ *vb* **snapped; snap·ping**
> **1** : to grasp or grasp at something suddenly with the mouth or teeth ⟨fish *snapping* at the bait⟩ **2** : to grasp at something eagerly ⟨*snapped* at the chance to go⟩ **3** : to get, take, or buy at once ⟨*snap* up a bargain⟩ **4** : to speak or utter sharply or irritably ⟨*snap* out a command⟩ **5** : to break or break apart suddenly and often with a cracking noise ⟨the branch *snapped*⟩ **6** : to make or cause to make a sharp or crackling sound ⟨*snap* a whip⟩ **7** : to close or fit in place with a quick movement ⟨the lid *snapped* shut⟩ **8** : to put into or remove from a position suddenly or with a snapping sound ⟨*snap* off a switch⟩ **9** : to close by means of snaps or fasteners **10** : to act or be acted on with snap ⟨*snapped* to attention⟩ **11** : to take a snapshot of

Which Phrase Fits?

Pick the verbal illustration that is the best match for the meaning shown. Write the letter in the blank.

1. dishonest _____
   a) ⟨a *crooked* path⟩   b) ⟨the picture is *crooked*⟩   c) ⟨a *crooked* card game⟩

2. learn _____
   a) ⟨good readers *pick up* new words from their reading⟩
   b) ⟨*pick up* a bargain⟩   c) ⟨*picked up* the outlaw's trail⟩

pulley

33

© 2004 Merriam-Webster Inc.

Your name _____

3. to cause to ignite by scratching _____
    a) ⟨the ship *struck* a rock⟩   b) ⟨*strike* a match⟩   c) ⟨*strike* a bargain⟩

4. to provide temporary quarters for _____
    a) ⟨*lodge* a guest for the night⟩   b) ⟨we *lodged* in motels⟩   c) ⟨*lodge* a complaint⟩

5. not holding public office _____
    a) ⟨*private* property⟩   b) ⟨a *private* citizen⟩   c) ⟨a *private* meeting⟩

6. good working condition _____
    a) ⟨a list of names in alphabetical *order*⟩   b) ⟨the telephone is out of *order*⟩
    c) ⟨place an *order* for groceries⟩

Which Meaning Matches?

Pick the meaning that is the best match for the verbal illustration shown. Write the letter in the blank.

1. ⟨don't *scramble* up those papers⟩ _____
    a) to work hard to win or escape something   b) to mix together in disorder
    c) to cook eggs by stirring them while frying

2. ⟨an *original* mind⟩ _____
    a) of or relating to the origin or beginning   b) not copied from anything else
    c) able to think up new things

3. ⟨*plead* illness⟩ _____
    a) to argue for or against   b) to offer as an excuse or an apology
    c) to make an earnest appeal

4. ⟨we *split* the profit⟩ _____
    a) to divide lengthwise   b) to burst or break apart
    c) to divide into shares or sections

5. ⟨*hot* jewels⟩ _____
    a) recently stolen   b) radioactive   c) easily excited

6. ⟨*burned* my finger⟩ _____
    a) to destroy by fire or heat   b) to make or produce by fire or heat
    c) to injure by fire or heat

17 Usage Notes

quarterhorse

Your name _____

The *italic* usage labels that come before definitions and the verbal illustrations after the definitions are two ways that Merriam-Webster dictionaries give you extra information about how words are used. And there's a third way—**usage notes** following definitions. Usage notes are short phrases that are separated from the definition by a dash. They tell you how or when the entry word is used.

> **blast off** \blas-ˈtȯf\ *vb* : to take off — used of vehicles using rockets for power
> **cas·ta·net** \ˌkas-tə-ˈnet\ *n* : a rhythm instrument that consists of two small ivory, wooden, or plastic shells fastened to the thumb and clicked by the fingers in time to dancing and music — usually used in plural
> ²**cheer** *vb*... **4** : to grow or be cheerful — usually used with *up*

castanet

The usage note at **blast off** tells you that the word is usually used in a particular situation. The note at **castanet** tells you that the word is most often used in the plural form and with a plural verb, although it is defined as a singular. (If the word was *always* plural, it would have been entered as **castanets** and defined as plural.) Usage notes like the one at **cheer** tell you what words are usually used with the entry word in a sentence. In this case, the expression is usually *cheer up*.

Sometimes dictionaries use usage notes in place of definitions. This is done when the way the word is used is more important than what the word means.

> ²**both** *conj* — used before two words or phrases connected with *and* to stress that each is included ⟨*both* New York and London⟩

Usage notes are also used in place of a definition for interjections, which usually express a feeling or reaction to something rather than a meaning.

> **amen** \ˈā-ˈmen, ˈä-\ *interj* — used to express agreement (as after a prayer or a statement of opinion)

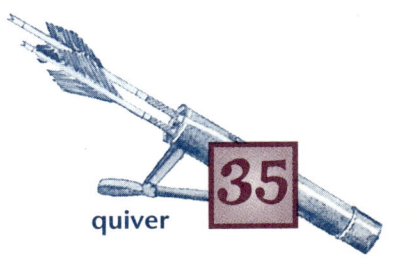

quiver

© 2004 Merriam-Webster Inc.

35

Your name _____

Usual Uses

For each definition, pick the form of the word that is most usual. Write the letter in the blank.

1. open seats for people to watch from _____
   a) bleacher   b) bleachers   c) Bleacher   d) Bleachers

2. an instrument with two adjustable legs _____
   a) Caliper   b) Calipers   c) caliper   d) calipers

3. to grow or be cheerful _____
   a) cheer around   b) cheer down   c) cheer up   d) cheer out

4. being a result _____
   a) due of   b) due from   c) due   d) due to

Using Usage

Choose the phrase that best completes the sentence. Write the letter in the blank.

1. The preposition *in* can be _____.
   a) used to show a state or condition   b) used to indicate a particular place or time
   c) used to show who or what is to receive something

2. The word *would* is often _____.
   a) capitalized   b) used with *up*   c) used to show politeness

3. The interjection *adios* is _____.
   a) used instead of hello   b) used instead of goodbye   c) used in France

4. The interjection *alas* is _____.
   a) used by pirates   b) used to express excitement and surprise
   c) used to express unhappiness, pity, or worry

© 2004 Merriam-Webster Inc.

18 Undefined Entries

rhinoceros

Your name _____

Some entries in the dictionary have boldface words at the end, like at the entry **amphibious**.

> ¹**am·phib·i·ous** \am-ˈfib-e-əs\ *adj* **1** : able to live both on land and in water ⟨*amphibious* animals⟩ **2** : meant to be used on both land and water ⟨*amphibious* vehicles⟩ **3** : made by land, sea, and air forces acting together ⟨*amphibious* attack⟩ — **am·phib·i·ous·ly** *adj* — **am·phib·i·ous·ness** *n*

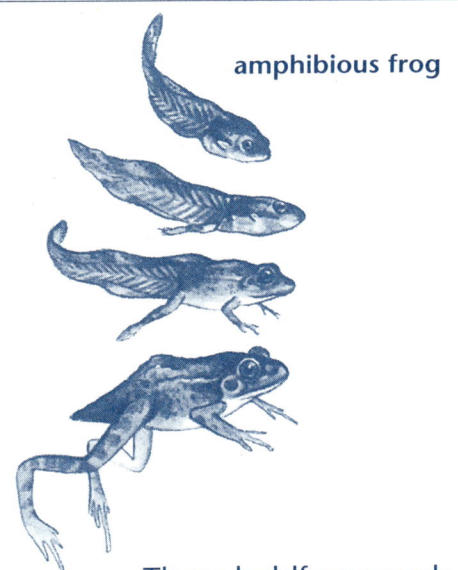

amphibious frog

These boldface words are **undefined run-on entries**. Each is shown without a definition of its own, but you can easily discover the meaning by simply combining the meaning of the base word (the main entry) and the added-on part (the suffix). For example, **amphibiously** is simply **amphibious** plus **-ly** ("in a specified manner") and so means "in an amphibious manner"; and **amphibiousness** is **amphibious** plus **-ness** ("state : condition") and so means "the state or condition of being amphibious."

Another example of an undefined entry is at the entry for **meat**.

> **meat** \ˈmēt\ *n* **1** : solid food ⟨*meat* and drink⟩ **2** : the part of something that can be eaten ⟨nut *meats*⟩ **3** : animal and especially mammal tissue for use as food **4** : the most important part : SUBSTANCE ⟨the *meat* of the story⟩ — **meat·less** \-les\ *adj*

The suffix **-less** means "not having," so **meat** plus **-less** means "not having any meat."

Your dictionary includes as run-on entries only words whose meanings you should have no trouble figuring out. If a word comes from a main entry plus a suffix but has a meaning that is not easy to understand from the meanings of the two parts, the dictionary will enter and define it at its own alphabetical place.

rattlesnake

© 2004 Merriam-Webster Inc.

Words Plus

Each of the words below is entered as a run-on entry of a main entry word in your dictionary. Match the words to the definitions in the right column. Write the number of the correct definition in the blank before the word.

___ baldness
___ bravely
___ copiously
___ fruitlessly
___ genuineness
___ guileful
___ hairless
___ intelligibly
___ invisibly
___ judiciously
___ juggler
___ lavishly
___ lopsidedness
___ motherhood
___ nonsensically
___ observantly
___ prowler
___ quibbler
___ ruthlessness
___ scatterbrained
___ stalked
___ timidly
___ uncivilly
___ valueless

1. without a threadlike growth from the skin of a person or lower animal
2. the state or condition of being cruel
3. in a manner that is impossible to see
4. the state or condition of lacking a natural covering
5. one who finds fault especially over unimportant points
6. having a slender supporting structure
7. one who moves about quietly and secretly like a wild animal hunting prey
8. in a manner characterized by good judgment
9. in an abundant manner
10. in a manner possible to understand
11. not having worth, usefulness, or importance in comparison with something else
12. in a manner that makes no sense
13. in an unsuccessful manner
14. characterized by sly trickery
15. in an impolite manner
16. in a manner suggesting a lack of fear
17. in a watchful manner
18. in an extravagant manner
19. having the characteristics of a flighty, thoughtless person
20. the state or condition of being just what it seems to be
21. the state or condition of being a female parent
22. in a manner suggesting a lack of courage or self-confidence
23. one who keeps several things moving in the air at the same time
24. the state or condition of being unbalanced

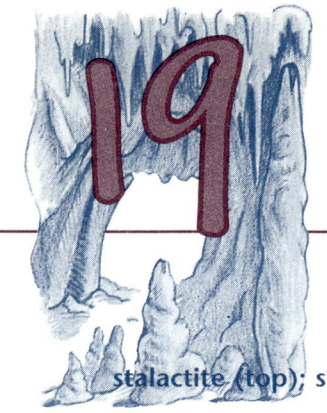

19 Synonym Paragraphs

Your name _____

stalactite (top); stalagmite (bottom)

In lesson 15 we discussed how synonyms (words that have the same or nearly the same meaning) appear in some definitions in SMALL CAPITAL letters. Merriam-Webster dictionaries handle synonyms in another way too. At the end of some entries, you will see a special kind of cross-reference like the one at **superb**.

---

su·perb \su̇-ˈpərb\ *adj* : outstandingly excellent, impressive, or beautiful **synonyms** see SPLENDID

The direction "**synonyms** see SPLENDID" means "for a discussion of synonyms that includes **superb**, see the entry **splendid**." Such discussions of synonyms are called **synonym paragraphs**.

Synonyms can often be substituted freely for one another in a sentence because they mean basically the same thing. Sometimes synonyms have meanings that are almost the same, but not exactly. They cannot always be substituted for one another. Synonyms may differ slightly in what they suggest to the reader—in the image they call to mind. These suggested meanings may make one synonym a better choice than another in certain situations.

Synonym paragraphs explain the little differences between synonyms. Any of the three words in the paragraph following the entry **splendid** would be satisfactory in the examples given to indicate something impressive. But over the years people have come to think of the word *glorious* as more suited to describing something where light or beauty is involved, while *splendid* and *superb* are used of other things. And something described as superb is often thought of as more wonderful than something merely splendid.

---

splen·did \ˈsplen-dəd\ *adj* **1** : having or showing splendor : BRILLIANT **2** : impressive in beauty, excellence, or magnificence ⟨did a *splendid* job⟩ ⟨a *splendid* palace⟩ **3** : GRAND **4** — **splen·did·ly** *adv*

synonyms SPLENDID, GLORIOUS, and SUPERB mean very impressive. SPLENDID suggests that something is far above the ordinary in excellence or magnificence ⟨what a *splendid* idea⟩ ⟨a *splendid* jewel⟩. GLORIOUS suggests that something is radiant with light or beauty ⟨a *glorious* sunset⟩. SUPERB suggests the highest possible point of magnificence or excellence ⟨a *superb* museum⟩ ⟨the food was *superb*⟩.

---

scorpion

© 2004 Merriam-Webster Inc.

Your name _____

Shades of Meaning

Find the synonym paragraph in your dictionary for each set of words listed below. Read the paragraph carefully, then choose the word that is the best fit for each sentence.

> enjoyment, joy, pleasure / mend, patch, repair
> calm, peaceful, tranquil / task, duty, job

1. Her face was shining with _____ after learning that she had won the contest.

   He takes personal _____ in doing a good job.

   The bad weather did not take away from our _____ of the picnic.

2. The old clock took many hours to _____.

   I thought my favorite jeans were ruined forever, but Mom showed me how to _____ the hole with a scrap of material.

   I'll have to _____ that dress if I want to wear it to the wedding.

3. The _____ beauty of a mountain view always puts me in a relaxed mood.

   It is important to remain _____ in an emergency.

   We enjoyed a _____ dinner after the fussy children went to bed.

4. We will have to work hard if we want to get the _____ done in time.

   The teacher assigned me the _____ of collecting everyone's assignments.

   If you have a pet, it is your _____ to be responsible and take good care of it.

© 2004 Merriam-Webster Inc.

20 Phrases

teepee

Your name _____

The last kind of **boldface** entry you will find in your Merriam-Webster dictionary is the **defined run-on phrase**. These phrases are groups of words that, when used together, have a special meaning that is more than just the sum of the ordinary meanings of each word.

> ¹**stand** \'stand\ *vb* **stood** \'stu̇d\; **stand·ing 1 :** to be in or take a vertical position on one's feet **2 :** to take up or stay in a specified position or condition ⟨*stands* first in the class⟩ ⟨*stands* accused⟩ ⟨machines *standing* idle⟩ **3 :** to have an opinion ⟨how do you *stand* on taxes?⟩ **4 :** to rest, remain, or set in a usually vertical position ⟨*stand* the box in the corner⟩ **5 :** to be in a specified place ⟨the house stands on the hill⟩ **6 :** to stay in effect ⟨the order still *stands*⟩ **7 :** to put up with : ENDURE ⟨can't *stand* pain⟩ **8 :** UNDERGO ⟨*stand* trial⟩ **9 :** to perform the duty of ⟨*stand* guard⟩ — **stand by :** to be or remain loyal or true to ⟨*stand by* a promise⟩ — **stand for 1 :** to be a symbol for : REPRESENT **2 :** to put up with : PERMIT ⟨won't *stand for* any nonsense⟩

The defined run-on phrases are placed at the end of the entry that is the first major word of the phrase. Normally this will be the first noun or verb rather than an adjective or preposition. The phrases run on at **stand** all begin with the entry word **stand**. But some run-on phrases will not have the major word at the beginning of the phrase. Keep in mind that the phrase will be entered at the first major word in the phrase. This word is usually a noun or a verb. Where do you think you would find the phrases **out of the blue, at any rate, by hand,** and **take care of**? If you said at the noun **blue**, at the noun **rate**, at the noun **hand**, and at the verb **take**, then you understand where you should look for the phrases.

Where to find the phrase **read between the lines** may puzzle you at first, since it contains both a verb (**read**) and a noun (**lines**). But if you remember that the phrase will be entered at the *first* major word, in this case the verb **read**, you should have no trouble finding the phrases entered in this dictionary.

by hand

trout

© 2004 Merriam-Webster Inc.

Your name _____

Eureka!

Here are some run-on phrases from your dictionary. In the blank next to each phrase write the main entry word where you found the phrase.

_____ 1. put forward

_____ 2. out of the blue

_____ 3. take part

_____ 4. in spite of

_____ 5. from time to time

_____ 6. get one's goat

_____ 7. make believe

_____ 8. in common

_____ 9. beside oneself

_____ 10. on the contrary

_____ 11. turn the trick

_____ 12. out of hand

_____ 13. play hooky

_____ 14. follow suit

_____ 15. on the spot

_____ 16. by no means

What Does It Mean?

Pick the choice that gives the correct meaning for the following run-on phrases. Write the letter in the blank.

1. get ahead _____
    a) to buy property   b) to push and shove   c) to achieve success

2. better part _____
    a) more than half   b) superior component   c) favorite food

3. at every turn _____
    a) all the time   b) where to stop   c) the corners of a square figure

4. get wind of _____
    a) feel a draught   b) fly a kite   c) become aware of

5. set about _____
    a) place wickets on a croquet course   b) begin to do   c) run away

6. on tap _____
    a) liquid   b) inexpensive   c) available

7. read between the lines _____
    a) read carefully   b) hallucinate   c) understand more than is directly stated

21 Word History Paragraphs

unicorn

Your name _____

One of the important jobs of people who study words and write dictionaries is finding out where the words we use every day in English came from. Some of our words are made up by people using the language today. Whenever a scientist discovers a new element or creates a new drug, for example, he or she makes up a name for it.

But most of the words in the English language have a long history. They usually can be traced back to other words in languages older than English. Many of these languages, like ancient Greek and Latin, are no longer spoken today. The study of the origins of words can be fascinating, for many of our words have very interesting stories behind them.

Some Merriam-Webster dictionaries (especially those that have been published for young students) include special short **word history paragraphs** like the one at **surly**. These paragraphs discuss the interesting stories of word origins and trace the development of meanings over the years.

> **sur·ly** \ˈsər-lē\ *adj* **sur·li·er; sur·li·est**
> : having a mean rude disposition
> : UNFRIENDLY
>
> **Word History** The word *surly* comes from the word *sir*. Long ago, some Englishmen who had the title *Sir* became too proud of it. Such men were called *sirly*, a word that meant "overbearing" and "arrogant." Over the years the spelling changed to *surly* and came to be used of anyone who is rude and unfriendly.

Where in the World?

For each of the words that follow, write the language that was its *earliest* source.

1. _____ academy
2. _____ admiral
3. _____ zest
4. _____ bugle
5. _____ lord
6. _____ flamingo
7. _____ chameleon
8. _____ amethyst
9. _____ robot
10. _____ molar
11. _____ nickel
12. _____ gorgeous
13. _____ hazard
14. _____ lunatic
15. _____ dachshund
16. _____ uproar
17. _____ ballot
18. _____ December
19. _____ lady
20. _____ panic

umiak

© 2004 Merriam-Webster Inc.

Looking Back

Write the number of the correct description on the right next to each word on the left.

_____ ukulele   1. from a Spanish word meaning "a stray animal"

_____ magazine   2. from Latin, Spanish, and Italian for "wild ox"

_____ canary   3. from a Hawaiian word meaning "jumping flea"

_____ chameleon   4. named for what Romans called the "dog islands"

_____ dog days   5. from the sound it makes

_____ hippopotamus   6. from a Dutch word meaning "donkey"

_____ denim   7. based on the idea of someone slipping out of a cloak

_____ mustang   8. from a Latin word meaning "white"

_____ easel   9. from a Latin word meaning "flame"

_____ flamingo   10. from a Greek word meaning "little crane"

_____ leech   11. from the Greek for "river horse"

_____ lunatic   12. from Arabic and French sources that meant "storehouse"

_____ katydid   13. from Greek words meaning "on the ground" and "lion"

_____ candidate   14. from a French word meaning "to go over again with a harrow"

_____ rehearse   15. from the Latin word for "moon"

_____ escape   16. from the name of a city in France

_____ buffalo   17. from an old word meaning "doctor"

_____ geranium   18. named for the time of the rising of a star

Words in Action

In this lesson, you looked at many word history paragraphs. They show that English words come from many different languages and cultures. Make a poster showing the many languages and cultures that have given words to English.

How to Use Your Thesaurus

22 What is a Thesaurus?

viaduct   Your name _____

A **thesaurus** is basically a collection of word lists. The words are grouped together with other words that are either the same or opposite in meaning. A person usually uses a thesaurus when he or she has one word in mind and is looking for a word that is like it or in direct contrast to it.

Some of the words grouped together in a thesaurus are very similar to one another. Others are alike in some ways and not in others. For example, at the thesaurus entry **car** you will find the words *auto* and *automobile*. Both of these are very close to *car* in meaning. But you will also find words like *sedan* and *station wagon*. These words are used for specific types of cars. You might also find a word like *jalopy*, which can refer to a car in a particular condition (a shabby old automobile). The same basic idea applies to opposite words. You will find some words that are exactly opposite and some that are almost opposite.

Some of the things you've learned about Merriam-Webster dictionaries also apply to Merriam-Webster thesauruses. The entries of the thesaurus are arranged in alphabetical order. Each entry is introduced by a **boldface** word that sticks out a bit into the margin. You will see *italic* functional labels indicating how each entry word is used in a sentence, verbal illustrations in angle brackets ⟨ ⟩, and cross-reference words in SMALL CAPITAL letters directing you to other entries. Homographs (words that are spelled the same but come from different sources or have different part-of-speech labels) have separate entries. And entries for words having more than one meaning are divided into meaning groups (or senses) introduced by boldface numbers.

But thesaurus entries look quite different from dictionary entries in other ways. Here are some sample thesaurus entries.

> **often** *adv* many times ⟨I seem to stumble *often* when I try to walk in high heels⟩
> **Synonyms** constantly, continually, frequently, oft, oftentimes (or ofttimes), repeatedly
> **Related words** always, continuously, consistently, perpetually; afresh, again, anew; commonly, ordinarily, regularly, routinely; intermittently, periodically, recurrently; generally, usually
> **Phrases** again and again, over and over, time after time, time and again
> **Near antonyms** occasionally, sometimes, sporadically, never; once
> **Antonyms** infrequently, rarely, seldom
>
> **oftentimes** (or **ofttimes**) *adv* many times ⟨children *oftentimes* don't realize how quickly time passes⟩ *see* OFTEN

© 2004 Merriam-Webster Inc.

vole

Your name _____

The entry **often** is a **main entry**. Each main entry in the thesaurus is made up of a boldface entry word followed by a functional label, a meaning number if needed, a meaning core with a short verbal illustration, and a list of synonyms. Most of the time the main entry also includes other kinds of lists, as at **often**. (We'll explain about each kind of list in upcoming lessons.) **Oftentimes** is a **secondary entry**. Each secondary entry in the thesaurus includes a cross-reference that directs you to a main entry where you will find more information.

Find the Misfit

Each set of words below includes one word that would NOT likely show up in a thesaurus entry with the other words. Circle the word that doesn't fit the group. Remember that the words do not have to be exactly the same, but they should have something in common—or they may be opposites. Use your dictionary if you are uncertain about the meaning of any of the words.

1. tiny   teeny   tawny   huge   miniature
2. run   sprint   scamper   scrawl   scurry
3. criticize   blame   censor   condemn   saturate
4. engrave   carve   idolize   etch   inscribe
5. humble   vainglorious   conceited   identical   meek
6. commotion   illumination   agitation   turmoil   calm
7. disconsolate   downcast   happy   despondent   dexterous
8. ruthless   rural   urban   rustic   pastoral

Dictionary Versus Thesaurus

Will you find the following dictionary features in your thesaurus as well? Circle *yes* or *no*.

1. verbal illustrations   yes   no
2. pronunciation symbols   yes   no
3. sense numbers   yes   no
4. word history paragraphs   yes   no
5. homographs   yes   no
6. usage paragraphs   yes   no
7. cross-reference words   yes   no
8. alphabetical order   yes   no
9. functional labels   yes   no
10. meanings   yes   no

© 2004 Merriam-Webster Inc.

23 Meaning Cores and Verbal Illustrations

Your name _____

In lesson 22 we said that a thesaurus is basically a collection of word lists, but the primary entries in Merriam-Webster thesauruses also include short definitions, or **meaning cores**. The meaning core indicates the sense or area of meaning in which a group of words is synonymous.

> **excellence** *n* **1** exceptionally high quality ⟨the annual awards honor *excellence* in children's literature⟩
> **Synonyms** distinction, excellency, greatness, preeminence, superbness, superiority, supremacy
> **Related words** faultlessness, flawlessness, impeccability, perfection; goodness, value, worth; consequence, importance, notability
> **Near antonyms** averageness, badness, inferiority, mediocrity, ordinariness, worthlessness
> **2** a quality that gives something special worth ⟨the particular *excellence* of down in clothing and sleeping bags is its lightness⟩
> **Synonyms** distinction, excellency, merit, value, virtue
> **Related words** advantage, edge, superiority
> **Near antonyms** blemish, defect, failing, fault, flaw
> **Antonyms** deficiency

The meaning core for **excellence 2**, for example, is "a quality that gives something special worth." This is the meaning of *excellence* for which the words *distinction, excellency, merit, value,* and *virtue* are synonyms.

In some cases, a meaning core is followed by a typical object in parentheses.

> **express** *vb* to make known (as an idea, emotion, or opinion)

The material in parentheses in the entry **express** tells you that the word is usually used in connection with "an idea, emotion, or opinion."

Each meaning core in both main entries and secondary entries is followed by a verbal illustration enclosed in angle brackets.

> ⟨the particular *excellence* of down in clothing and sleeping bags is its lightness⟩

This verbal illustration shows a typical use of the entry word **excellence 2** in the sense defined by the meaning core.

49

Your name _____

Matchmaker
Match each meaning core on the left with a word on the right.
Write the number of the correct word in the blank.

_____ language, behavior, or ideas that are absurd and contrary to good sense

_____ to avoid by going around

_____ a giving or taking of one thing of value in return for another

_____ to subject (someone) to constant scoldings and sharp reminders

_____ of, relating to, or experienced through the sense of hearing

_____ to cause to cease burning

_____ one who operates or navigates a seagoing vessel

1. nag
2. extinguish
3. detour
4. aural
5. nonsense
6. mariner
7. trade

Matchmaker
Match each meaning core on the left with a verbal illustration on the right.
Write the number of the correct verbal illustration in the blank.

_____ filled with fear or dread

_____ harsh and dry in sound

_____ lacking fresh air

_____ a state or time of great activity, thriving, or achievement

_____ to drive or force out

_____ lacking bodily energy or motivation

_____ showing a natural kindness and courtesy

1. ⟨a lovely young man in the full *bloom* of youth⟩

2. ⟨I am *frightened* by the dark⟩

3. ⟨we quickly *ejected* the unwanted guest from our party⟩

4. ⟨a *gracious* teacher who made the new student feel welcome⟩

5. ⟨a few *languid* dancers swayed about the dance floor without much enthusiasm⟩

6. ⟨the dying man spoke in a *hoarse* whisper⟩

7. ⟨the house was *stuffy* after being closed up for a month⟩

© 2004 Merriam-Webster Inc.

24 Synonyms and Related Words

xylophone

Your name _____

The next part of the main entry of your thesaurus is the list of synonyms.

> **safety** *n* **1** the state of not being exposed to danger ⟨we were lucky to make it to *safety* just as the lions broke loose from their cage at the zoo⟩
> **Synonyms** protection, safeness, security

In Merriam-Webster thesauruses, synonyms are words that share a basic meaning with the entry word. The synonyms may have other meanings as well, but they must have at least one meaning in common with the entry word and the other synonyms in the list. The meaning core that comes before the synonym list tells you what meaning is shared by the words in the list.

In many entries, the synonym list is followed by a list of **related words**.

> **early** *adv* before the usual or expected time ⟨that year spring arrived *early*⟩
> **Synonyms** beforehand, inopportunely, precociously, prematurely, unseasonably
> **Related words** immediately, promptly, punctually; betimes, seasonably

Related words are words that are almost but not quite synonyms.

If you are looking for a word that is very close in meaning to a given word, the synonym list is the place to look. But if you are looking for a word that is only somewhat similar, you should look at the list of related words.

Bet on a Set

Select the set of synonyms that is the best match for each meaning core below. Write the appropriate letter in the blank.

1. a complete amount of something _____
    a) piece, portion, section   b) total, whole, entire   c) small, little, petite

2. lacking a definite plan, purpose, or pattern _____
    a) foolish, silly, witless   b) comic, funny, laughable   c) aimless, haphazard, random

3. requiring considerable physical or mental effort _____
    a) apt, likely, prone   b) arduous, hard, difficult
    c) petty, paltry, trivial

xebec

© 2004 Merriam-Webster Inc.

Your name _____

4. being less plentiful than what is normal, necessary, or desirable _____
   a) plaintive, mournful, melancholy   b) eloquent, expressive, significant
   c) scanty, skimpy, meager

5. to move or act slowly _____
   a) curtail, abridge, diminish   b) abrade, chafe, graze   c) dawdle, delay, loiter

6. to talk about (an issue) usually from various points of view and for the purpose of arriving at a decision or opinion _____
   a) bewilder, fluster, muddle   b) camouflage, cloak, mask   c) discuss, debate, argue

All in the Family

Select the set of related words that is the best match for the entry word below. Write the appropriate letter in the blank.

1. prevent _____
   a) break, crack, snap   b) baffle, foil, thwart   c) appreciate, comprehend, understand

2. hesitation _____
   a) doubt, delay, reluctance   b) aid, comfort, support   c) ascent, rise, pitch

3. laziness _____
   a) apathy, listlessness, languor   b) agony, distress, misery   c) bustle, bother, flurry

4. faithful _____
   a) dependable, trustworthy, determined   b) blithe, jovial, mirthful
   c) clean, fastidious, finicky

5. vitality _____
   a) brightness, cheer, eagerness   b) ability, competence, prowess
   c) articulation, voice, language

Words in Action

The Word Whiz is a comic strip superhero who uses lots of synonyms. Create a comic strip about The Word Whiz. Be sure to include plenty of synonyms in the strip!

© 2004 Merriam-Webster Inc.

25 Phrases

Your name _____

Phrases are idioms that have meanings that are different from the overall meaning of the words that make them up. For example, the phrase *a feather in one's cap* means "accomplishment"—but if you look up the entries *feather* and *cap* in the dictionary you won't find any definitions that explain the meaning of the phrase.

If a phrase has the same meaning as the words of a synonym group, it will be included in the thesaurus entry. In Merriam-Webster thesaurus entries, phrases are listed after the synonyms and the related words.

> **accomplishment** *n* a successful result brought about by hard work ⟨Jared's biggest *accomplishment* this week was finishing his art project⟩
> **Synonyms** achievement, attainment, coup, success, triumph
> **Related words** blockbuster, hit, jackpot, megahit, smash, winner, conquest, gain, victory, win; acquirement, skill; deed, feat, performance; completion, consummation, culmination, execution, fruition, fulfillment, implementation, realization
> **Phrases** a feather in one's cap

Some phrases are used in more than one form, such as *get a kick out of* and *get a charge out of* at the entry **enjoy**. When this happens the thesaurus will include the variant words in parentheses. Both forms are correct and you can use whichever you like best.

> **enjoy** *vb* to take pleasure in ⟨TV and videos are OK, but we still *enjoy* seeing movies on the big screen⟩
> **Synonyms** adore, delight (in), dig, fancy, groove (on), like, love, relish, revel (in)
> **Related words** admire, appreciate, cherish, revere, venerate, worship; prize, treasure, value; devour, drink (in), savor; dote (on), idolize; cotton (to), favor, prefer
> **Phrases** be partial to, get a kick (*or* charge) out of, go for, have a soft spot for, take to

© 2004 Merriam-Webster Inc.

Your name _____

One and the Same

On the bottom part of this page you will find a list of idioms and their meanings. Where would you expect to find each idiom entered in the thesaurus? Match each idiom to a word that shares its meaning in the list below. Write the number in the appropriate blank.

_____ frolic   _____ gasp   _____ escape

_____ make   _____ learn   _____ heal

_____ gather   _____ eager   _____ worry

_____ inspect   _____ idle   _____ poor

_____ immediately _____ fast   _____ eject

1. champing at the bit — showing urgent desire or interest
2. send packing — to drive or force out
3. by leaps and bounds — with great speed
4. kick up one's heels — to play and run about happily
5. to be out of breath — to breathe hard, quickly, or with difficulty
6. fly the coop — get free from a dangerous or confining situation
7. get together — to bring together in one body or place
8. go over — to look over closely (as for judging quality or condition)
9. take care of — to restore to a healthy condition
10. kill time — to spend time doing nothing
11. hard up — lacking money or material possessions
12. give a hang — to experience concern or anxiety
13. at once — without delay
14. get the hang of — to acquire complete knowledge, understanding, or skill in
15. put together — to bring into being by combining or shaping materials

Words in Action

The Phrase Fans Drama Club wants to produce a brand-new play that includes lots of phrases. They are asking writers to submit scripts for their new show. Choose five or six phrases from the One and the Same exercise in this lesson and write a play for the Phrase Fans show. When you are done, perform your play for the class.

26 Antonyms and Near Antonyms

Your name _____

In Merriam-Webster thesauruses, a word is an **antonym** when it has a basic meaning that is in direct contrast to the basic meaning of a synonym group. **Near antonyms** are words that are nearly opposite, but not quite. Often, near antonyms (also called *contrasted words*) differ from antonyms in emphasis or in the suggestions they communicate. For example, the word *poor* is the antonym of the word *rich* because its meaning is exactly opposite and because it is similarly matter-of-fact in tone. The word *broke* is a near antonym. It is close to *poor* in meaning but is more emphatic (it means "having no money") and it carries a stronger suggestion of distress.

In a Merriam-Webster thesaurus entry, the near antonyms and antonyms come after the synonyms, related words, and phrases. The near antonyms come before the antonyms.

> **last** *adj* following all others of the same kind in order or time <last one in the pool is a rotten *egg*>
> **Synonyms** closing, concluding, final, hindmost, latest, latter, rearmost, terminal, terminating, ultimate
> **Related words** consequent, ensuing, eventual, following, succeeding; conclusive, crowning, decisive, definitive; farthest, furthest, remotest; lowermost, lowest, nethermost; endmost, extreme, outermost, outmost; penultimate
> **Near antonyms** eminent, premier, superior
> **Antonyms** beginning, earliest, first, inaugural, initial, maiden, opening, original, primary, starting

Find the Antonym
Select the antonym for each of the words listed below. Write the letter of the antonym in the blank.

1. absent _____
   a) adrift   b) present   c) dependable

2. stiff _____
   a) imaginary   b) dense   c) floppy

3. talkative _____
   a) chatty   b) negative   c) reserved

4. extinct _____
   a) alive   b) fallen   c) melancholy

5. stylish _____
   a) urbane   b) genial   c) dowdy

6. doubtful _____
   a) questionable   b) certain   c) wrong

© 2004 Merriam-Webster Inc.

Your name _____

Find the Near Antonym
Select the word that contrasts with each of the words listed below. Write the letter of the near antonym in the blank.

1. downcast _____
    a) dejected   b) upland   c) uplifted

2. explicit _____
    a) obscure   b) certain   c) hydraulic

3. tearful _____
    a) sad   b) special   c) cheery

4. betray _____
    a) observe   b) tempt   c) protect

5. persevere _____
    a) secure   b) falter   c) transact

6. stingy _____
    a) selfish   b) kindly   c) shy

Opposites Attract
Draw lines to connect each word on the left to an antonym or near antonym on the right.

simplify	low
send	old-fashioned
mature	crawl
top	complicate
truth	optimist
approach	young
decrease	receive
pessimist	enlarge
run	dry
humid	retreat
modern	fiction

Words in Action
Writers use the thesaurus to help them find just the write word to use. It inspires them. Write a poem called *An Ode to the Thesaurus* that tells why it is so helpful. Don't forget to include some examples of synonyms and antonyms!

Vocabulary Building

Word Workout Exercises

Word History Detective

Your name _____

Word Workout: Vocabulary Builder 1

1. Read the sentence below. Look up the boldface word in your dictionary. Then answer the question that follows.

   Beth and I love to **banter**, but we're always careful not to hurt each other's feelings with our teasing.

   Which word below could be used to replace *banter* in the sentence above without changing the meaning of the sentence? Circle the letter in front of that word.

   A. vex   **B.** kid   **C.** clamor   **D.** whoop

2. Look up the two words below in your dictionary. Then answer the question that follows.

   capital   **capitol**

Read the sentences below. Rewrite the sentences so each one uses the word with the right meaning– *capital* or *capitol*—to make the sentence correct.

   A. Our teacher instructed us to write our names in all *capitols*.
   B. The encyclopedia says that Ottawa is the *capitol* of Canada.
   C. The Chairman proposed investing some of the company's *capitol* in computers.
   D. The governor is sworn in on the steps of the state *capito*l.

A. _____

B. _____

C. _____

D. _____

3. Some *insects*, such as wasps and bees, are related to each other. Related insects often look alike. Some words are also related, and related words often look alike too. Look up the word *insect* in your dictionary. Then answer the question that follows.

   Which of the following words do you think is related to the word *insect* (that is, which word do you think has the same ancestor words as *insect*)? Circle the letter in front of that word.

   A. section   **B.** bug   **C.** security   **D.** insist

Word History Detective:
The Case of the Lily-Livered Varmint

"All right, you **lily-livered** varmint," yelled the sheriff, "stop hiding and come out with your hands up!" Why do you think cowardly folks are called *lily-livered*? Look up the term in the dictionary. Then write a paragraph explaining why cowards (and varmints) are called *lily-livered*.

© 2004 Merriam-Webster Inc.

Your name _____

Word Workout: Vocabulary Builder 2

1. Read the paragraph below. Then answer the question that follows.

   1 In 1863, Abraham Lincoln issued an order he called the **E-**
   2 **mancipation** Proclamation. It is one of the most famous
   3 documents in American history. It ordered states that were
   4 not part of the Union of the United States to free – or **em-**
   5 **ancipate**—their slaves. When Lincoln issued the law of **eman-**
   6 **cipation**, he started the process of giving African American people
   7 their freedom and their rights. Later, in 1865, Congress **emanc-**
   8 **ipated** slaves in all states by passing the Thirteenth Amendment to
   9 the Constitution.

   Each line of the paragraph has a number next to it. Between which two lines are hyphens used correctly to divide a word into parts?

   A. In the word *emancipation* between lines 1 and 2
   B. In the word *emancipate* between lines 4 and 5
   C. In the word *emancipation* between lines 5 and 6
   D. In the word *emancipated* between lines 7 and 8

2. Read the sentence below. Look up the boldfaced word in your dictionary. Then answer the question that follows.

   Kendall tried several different ways of explaining the math formulas, but they remained an *enigma* to his best friend Dylan.

   Which word below could be used to replace *enigma* in the sentence above without changing the meaning of the sentence? Circle the letter in front of that word.

   A. muscadine   **B.** pommel   **C.** conundrum   **D.** antipathy

3. The word *incognito* can be used as an adjective or an adverb. Look up the word in your dictionary. Then read the sentences below. Which sentence correctly uses *incognito* as an adverb?

   A. LeDonna decided to wear an *incognito* costume to avoid being recognized.
   B. We traveled *incognito*, pretending to be Mr. and Mrs. John Smith.
   C. Allan wrote a book about his *incognito* wanderings through Paris.
   D. She bought an *incognito* yesterday, but she has broken it already.

Word History Detective:
The Case of the Eavesdropper

"I didn't mean to *eavesdrop*," said Darla apologetically, "but I overheard you say you're planning a surprise party for Kate and I wondered if I could help." Who or what do you think the original *eavesdropper* was? Look up the term in the dictionary. Then write a paragraph explaining where *eavesdropper* comes from.

Your name _____

Word Workout: Vocabulary Builder 3

1. Look up the word *copious* in the dictionary. Then read the sentences below. Which sentence uses the word *copious* correctly?

    A. Sharon was warned not to *copious*, but she looked at our test papers anyway.
    B. Nothing bothers Jamie—he's the most *copious* person I know.
    C. My grandmother is very *copious* and goes to church every week.
    D. There were *copious* amounts of food at the party, and I tried all the goodies.

2. Look up the word *attribute* in the dictionary. Then read the sentences below. On the basis of what you found out in the dictionary, which sentence is true?

    A. The word *attribute* is always used as an adjective and it is sometimes capitalized.
    B. *Attribute* is pronounced one way when it is used as a noun and a different way when it is used as a verb.
    C. The word *attribute* means exactly the same thing as the words *attributer* and *attribution*.
    D. *Attribute* is used mostly in British English, while U.S. speakers usually use the word *attribution* instead.

3. Read the sentence below. Look up the boldface word in your dictionary. Then answer the question that follows.

    Caitlyn never went into her bug-loving brother's room because she never new what kind of slimy, creepy, crawling creatures she might find **lurking** in there.

    Which of the following words could be used to replace *lurking* in the sentence above without changing the meaning of the sentence?

    A. skulking
    B. irking
    C. bleating
    D. flanking

Word History Detective:
The Case of the Guillotine's Name

In Charles Dickens' book *A Tale of Two Cities*, Sydney Carton takes his friend's place at the **guillotine**, saying, "It is a far, far better thing that I do, than I have ever done…." How did the *guillotine* get its name? Look up the term in the dictionary. Then write a paragraph telling how it was named. Then write your own sentence demonstrating the meaning of the word *guillotine*.

© 2004 Merriam-Webster Inc.

Your name _____

Word Workout: Vocabulary Builder 4

1. Read the paragraph below, then answer the question that follows.

The adjective *mercurial*, the name of the planet *Mercury*, and the name of the element *mercury* all come from the name of the Roman god Mercury, who was the messenger of the Roman gods. Mercury had to zip from place to place delivering messages, and he had a reputation for being very fast. Words based on his name are often used for speedy things. The planet Mercury, the innermost one in the solar system, is the fastest, traveling around the sun in only 88 days. The element mercury, also known as "quicksilver," is a liquid metal that skitters away rapidly when touched.

Look up *mercurial* in the dictionary. Based on the paragraph above and the definition you find in your dictionary, which sentence below best describes someone who is *mercurial*?

    A. A *mercurial* person must have silvery colored hair.
    B. Someone who is *mercuial* is very calm all the time.
    C. A *mercurial* person's moods change quickly and unpredictably.
    D. Someone who is *mercurial* has a good sense of humor and is very funny.

2. Look up the word **object** in the dictionary. *Object* developed from the Latin word *obicere*. Based on the definition of *object*, what do you think *obicere* means?

    A. to talk very loudly
    B. to be aware of
    C. to weep or cry
    D. to throw in the way of

3. Look up the word **reverie** in the dictionary. Which of the following topics is most likely to be the subject of a *reverie*?

    A. going on vacation
    B. mowing the lawn
    C. studying for a test
    D. walking the dog

Word History Detective:
The Case of the Grotesque Grotto

There's something *grotesque* about the paintings on the walls in some ancient ruins. There's something *grotesque* about some old caves. What do paintings and caves have to do with the history of the word *grotesque*? Look up the history of the word *grotesque* in the dictionary. Write a paragraph explaining how ancient Roman ruins, wall paintings, and caves are connected to the word.

© 2004 Merriam-Webster Inc.

Your name _____

Word Workout: Vocabulary Builder 5

1. Look up the two words below in your dictionary. Then answer the question that follows.

    discreet   *discrete*

   Fill in the blanks using either *discreet* or *discrete* to complete each sentence below correctly.

   A. To keep her homework organized, Isabel used _____ sections in her notebook for each subject.

   B. The coach was always very _____ , refusing to discuss why a player didn't make the team.

   C. Each lab partner was instructed to complete a _____ step in the experiment.

   D. Although Kevin and Kyle were twins, they had very different personalities and _____ interests.

2. If you have always thought that the word *silhouette* looks French, that's because the word comes into English from French. Look up *silhouette* in the dictionary. What was the origin of the word?

   A. It means "little shadow" in French.
   B. It comes from the artists' tool used to make a silhouette.
   C. It was the name of a stingy French government official.
   D. It comes from the words of a popular French song.

3. Look up the word *vaccine* in the dictionary. Then answer this question. Which animal played the biggest role in the development of the word *vaccine*?

   A. sheep
   B. cows
   C. chickens
   D. horses

Word History Detective:
The Case of the Baffling Buccaneer

Why did English speakers start calling pirates **buccaneers**? Look up the word *buccaneer* in the dictionary. Look it up in the thesaurus too. Then write a paragraph telling how pirates came to be called *buccaneers*. List some of the other words used as synonyms of *buccaneer* too.

© 2004 Merriam-Webster Inc.

Your name _____

Word Workout: Vocabulary Builder 6

1. When Dylan gave up his long-time ponytail for a buzz cut, Zack was so surprised he blurted out, "Whoa, **dude**, what happened to your head?!" *Dude* is a surprising word. What do you think it meant originally?

    A. A cowboy going on a cattle drive.
    B. A soldier in World War I.
    C. A surfer in California.
    D. A man who pays too much attention to his clothes.

2. Look up the words *frequent* and *frequently* in the dictionary. Then read each sentence below. Use either *frequent* or *frequently* to fill in each blank. Be sure to use the correct part of speech.

    A. I like to read so I _____ the library.
    B. Jamie _____ uses the phone to call her friends.
    C. Mr. Allen _____ golfs in his spare time.
    D. Our grandparents visit our house _____.

3. Look up the following words in the dictionary and thesaurus. Then answer the question that follows.

    rebuke   reprimand   admonish   chide

    Which of the four words above would be the best word to use to fill in the blank in the sentence below? Write a sentence telling why you think that word is the best one to use.

    The teacher _____ the students after she found out they broke the school's rules by sneaking their pet rat into class.

    _____
    _____
    _____
    _____

Word History Detective:
The Case of the Bunk Debunked

After watching the latest TV shows about UFOs, I was sure UFOs existed, but Grandpa just shook his head and snorted, "All that UFO stuff is a bunch of bunk!" A particular person and place gave English the word **bunk**. Look up the word in the dictionary. Then write a paragraph telling the true story of the history of *bunk*.

© 2004 Merriam-Webster Inc.

Your name _____

Word Workout: Vocabulary Builder 7

1. You don't need a mathematical formula to figure out the meanings of **calculate**. The meanings all add up once you know the word's origin. Which of these everyday items has the most to do with the history of the word *calculate*?

    A. bubbles
    B. pebbles
    C. brambles
    D. cables

2. The word **equinox** developed from two Latin parent words, *aequus* and *nox*. Look up *equinox* in the dictionary. Given what that word means, what do you think its parent words mean?

    A. *aequus* means "horse" and nox means "name."
    B. *aequus* means "water," and nox means "to come to know."
    C. *aequus* means "out of," and nox means "harm."
    D. *aequus* means "equal," and nox means "night."

3. Read the paragraph below, then answer the question that follows.

    The words **opinion, view, belief,** and **conviction** all mean something that you think is true. *Opinion* and *view* suggest a judgment that may not be shared by everyone (as in, "she shares my *opinion* of the movie" and "his *views* on the book differ from mine"). *Belief* suggests a view that you have come to accept fully in your own mind (as in, "she has a firm *belief* in the benefits of chocolate"). *Conviction* suggests an unchangeable belief (as in, "his *convictions* about music come from many years of study").

    Write four sentences that show the correct way to use the words *opinion, view, belief,* and *conviction*. Use one of those words in each sentence.

    _____
    _____
    _____
    _____

Word History Detective:
The Case of the Fabulous Tabby

A common housecat is just a plain, ordinary striped kitty. Or is she? There's more than meets the eye in the apparently average feline we call a **tabby**. Investigate how the *tabby* got her name. Write a paragraph telling how cats came to be called *tabbies*.

© 2004 Merriam-Webster Inc.

Your name _____

Word Workout: Vocabulary Builder 8

1. Look up the word *expedition* in your dictionary. Which of the following sentences uses the word *expedition* correctly?

    A. Profits from the bake sale did not meet our *expeditions.*
    B. The local library displayed an *expedition* of drawings by art students from our school.
    C. The playground at our school is a vast *expedition* of grass fields.
    D. On our *expedition* to the woods, we found a new path we had never seen before.

2. Look up *console* in the dictionary. Then read the example sentence below and answer the question that follows.

    I ran over to *console* Marcia after she bumped into the television and broke the knob off the *console.*

    Which of the following statements about the sentence above is true?

    A. The sentence uses *console* as a noun, but that word should only be used as a verb.
    B. The noun *console* should be replaced with the noun *construct* to make the sentence correct.
    C. The sentence uses both the noun *console* and the verb *console* correctly.
    D. The verb *console* should be replaced with the verb confirm to make the sentence correct.

3. Bang! R-r-ring! Gobble. Whiz. Splash. Snap. Whippoorwill. Plop! All of those words sound like the thing they name. There is a special name for the process of forming a word by imitating a sound. Which of the following words correctly names the process of forming words like *hiss* or *buzz*?

    A. onomatopoeia
    B. articulation
    C. calliope
    D. interference

Word History Detective:
The Case of the Bothersome Boycott

In the late 1870s and early 1880s, there was trouble in Ireland. It was a problem that cost farmers dearly, but it enriched the English language by adding the word **boycott.** Look up the word *boycott* in the dictionary. Write a paragraph explaining how a historical problem in Ireland gave rise to the word.

Your name _____

Word Workout: Vocabulary Builder 9

1. Look up the word **vehement**. Then read the four sentences below. Which sentence below uses *vehement* correctly? Write which sentence you picked and tell why you think that one is right.

   A. The library is always the most *vehement* place to study.
   B. My sister denied that she had eaten the last *vehement*.
   C. David asked if he could use the *vehement* to go to the baseball game.
   D. Bud and Joey had a *vehement* debate about whose soccer team is best.

   _____
   _____
   _____
   _____

2. Read the sentence below. Look up the boldface word in your dictionary. Then answer the question that follows.

   Everyone at the pizzeria was amazed to see how easily Francesca could **manipulate** a lump of sticky dough and turn it into a thin, perfectly shaped crust.

   Which word could be used to replace manipulate in the sentence above without changing the meaning of the sentence?

   A. examine
   B. continue
   C. open
   D. handle

3. English has plenty of ways to say "having a bad smell." One word that says "stinky" is *putrid*. Which other word below is a synonym of *putrid*?

   A. luxurious
   B. fleecy
   C. clumsy
   D. rank

Word History Detective:
The Case of the Colorful Khaki

Does the word **khaki** make you think of ancient Greeks in togas? Or Native Americans riding the open range? Or Chinese explorers trekking through the mountains? Or residents of India strolling through dusty city streets? Look up *khaki* in the dictionary, then write a paragraph telling about the history of the word.

Your name _____

Word Workout: Vocabulary Builder 10

1. Read the sentence below. Then answer the question that follows.

   "We snatched on a few odds and ends of clothing, *cocooned* ourselves in the proper red blankets, and plunged along the halls and out into the whistling wind bareheaded." (from *A Tramp Abroad* by Mark Twain).

   Which of the following statements about the sentence above is true?

   A. In the sentence, *cocoon* is a noun meaning "a silky covering for caterpillars."
   B. In the sentence, *cocoon* is a noun meaning "a home for butterflies."
   C. In the sentence, *cocoon* is a verb meaning "to wrap yourself up tightly."
   D. In the sentence, *cocoon* is a verb meaning "to run away."

2. Read the paragraph below. Then answer the question that follows.

   When an animal is frightened, it may "turn tail" and run away. A frightened dog tucks its tail between its legs and runs. There is also a traditional belief that cowards hide in the back or at the "tail end" of an advancing army. Perhaps some or all of these factors influenced early French speakers to adapt their word *coe*, meaning "tail" (from Latin *cauda*, "tail") into a new word, *coart*, which names people who are easily frightened. By the thirteenth century, *coart* had been borrowed into English, where its spelling and pronunciation were changed. It eventually became our word **coward**.

   Based on the information in the paragraph above, which of the following statements is true?

   A. The English word *coward* and the French word *coe* mean the same thing.
   B. The English word *tail* and the French word *coart* mean the same thing.
   C. The English word *coward* developed from the French word *coart*.
   D. The English word *coward* is older than the French word *coe*.

3. Which two words below are synonyms of the word **common**?

   A. *unwieldy* and *huge*
   B. *ordinary* and *familiar*
   C. *frustrated* and *angry*
   D. *fastidious* and *tidy*

Word History Detective:
The Case of the Dastardly Date

It's time to point the finger at the source of the English noun *date*. Where did it come from? How did it end up in English? Be careful in your investigation! We want to know the history of the word *date* that names the brownish fruit—not the *date* you find on a calendar page or the kind you go on with a friend. Write a paragraph telling about the origins of the word *date*.

Your name _____

Word Workout: Vocabulary Builder 11

1. Look up the word **ostensibly**. Then read the sentences below. Which sentence uses ostensibly correctly?

    A. The book was *ostensibly* written in the future to make the story seem more real.
    B. She laughed *ostensibly* at the silly antics of the cartoon characters.
    C. We all ran *ostensibly* up the hill, pulling our sleds behind us.
    D. The box was so *ostensibly* heavy I had trouble carrying it up the stairs.

2. Read the paragraph below. Then answer the question that follows.

Jade and other gemstones were once believed to cure sickness. Jade was supposed to be especially good at curing kidney problems. In the 16th century, the Spanish brought jade back from the New World. The Spanish named the gemstone *piedra de la ijada* (meaning "loin stone") because of their belief that jade could cure kidney disease. Eventually, jade became popular throughout western Europe both for wearing as jewelry and for curing or preventing disease. French speakers began using the last word in the Spanish name, spelling it *ejade*, and later, *jade*. English took its word for the gemstone directly from the French.

Which list below correctly shows the languages that the ancestors of the word *jade* passed through as it developed into the word we use today?

    A. Spanish → French → English
    B. French → Spanish → English
    C. Spanish → English → French → English
    D. French → English → Spanish → English

3. The word **xylophone** is made up of two parts, *xylo* and *phon*. Both of those parts come from Greek words. Look up *xylophone*. Based on what *xylophone* means, what do you think *xylo* and *phon* mean?

    A. "music" and "loud"
    B. "old" and "flat"
    C. "heavy" and "drum"
    D. "wood" and "sound"

Word History Detective:
The Case of the Insidious Influenza

When people get sick, do the stars have anything to do with it? Or did something else give the disease we call **influenza** its bad name? Look up *influenza*. Then write a paragraph explaining how the word developed and spread through English.

© 2004 Merriam-Webster Inc.

Your name _____

Word Workout: Vocabulary Builder 12

1. Look up the word *demure*. Then read the sentences below. Which sentence uses *demure* correctly?

    A. Greg was *demure* when he won the prize, telling everyone he didn't deserve it.
    B. George really made me *demure* when he said that I was being too loud.
    C. Claudia gave a *demure* speech that got everyone at the football rally excited.
    D. Kathy was so *demure* when she got her new kitten that she jumped for joy.

2. Look up *embrace* in the dictionary. Note that it can be used as two different parts of speech and it has several meanings. Write four sentences on the lines below to show four different meanings of the word *embrace*.

    _____
    _____
    _____
    _____

3. Read the sentence below. Look up the boldface term in your dictionary. Then answer the question that follows.

    Finding the combination to the door lock in the computer game was tricky, and Jackie spent an hour trying to **puzzle** out a solution to get it open.

    What does *puzzle* mean in the sentence above?

    A. a question, problem, or device intended to test someone's skill or cleverness
    B. something that is confusing or tricky
    C. to confuse
    D. to solve by thought or by clever guessing

Word History Detective:
The Case of the Perfect Pupil

Can you see yourself working as a private eye? Then cast your detective's glance into the dictionary and uncover the history of the word *pupil*. Does the name of the *pupil* in the eye have anything in common with the *pupils* that fill chairs at school? Write a paragraph that unveils the mystery of that word's history.

70

© 2004 Merriam-Webster Inc.

Your name _____

Word Workout: Vocabulary Builder 13

1. Read the sentences below. Look up the boldfaced term in your dictionary. Then answer the question that follows.

   Grandma came out to the porch, threw me a dish towel, and said, "Quit **lounging** around out here! Get in there and dry those dishes!"

   Which of the following correctly tells what the word *lounging* means in the sentence above?

   A. a long couch
   B. a room with comfortable furniture
   C. moving or acting in a lazy, slow, or tired manner : loafing
   D. feeling warm affection for : liking very much

2. Read the sentence below. Look up the boldfaced term in your dictionary. Then answer the question that follows.

   Did you know that July 2 is "I Forgot Day," and on that date, you can send a birthday card to **compensate** for missing someone's birthday earlier in the year?

   Which word below could be used to replace *compensate* in the sentence above without changing the meaning of the sentence?

   A. recompense   B. reconnoiter   C. reconstruct   D. recommend

3. Read the paragraph below, then answer the question that follows.

   In the book *Gulliver's Travels,* British author Jonathan Swift describes the island of Lilliput. The island is populated by people who only grow to be six inches tall. Swift used the Lilliputians to poke fun at conditions in England during the 1700s, comparing the ridiculous behavior of the tiny people to that of his countrymen.

   The English word **lilliputian** comes from the name of the people of Lilliput in Jonathan Swift's book. Based on the information in the paragraph, what do you think *lilliputian* means in English?

   A. ridiculous, silly
   B. small, miniature
   C. fast, quick
   D. mysterious, secretive

Word History Detective:
The Case of the Tantalized King

When something is *tantalizing,* you want it very much—but you just can't have it. How could a word end up with such a teasing, tormenting meaning? Look up the word *tantalize* in the dictionary. Then write a paragraph revealing the fruit of your labor, telling the tale of the history of *tantalize* once and for all!

© 2004 Merriam-Webster Inc.

Your name _____

Word Workout: Vocabulary Builder 14

1. Someone who is *nonchalant* appears calm, cool, and collected. Which of these other words can also describe someone like that?

    A. composed
    B. agitated
    C. melancholy
    D. exuberant

2. Read the paragraph below. Then answer the question that follows.

The words **hinder, impede, obstruct,** and **block** all suggest interfering with progress or with an activity. Use *hinder* to stress delaying progress in a harmful or annoying way (as in, "the heavy rain *hindered* the climb"). Choose *impede* to imply making progress difficult by clogging or hampering (as in, "tight clothing *impedes* movement"). Pick *obstruct* to suggest interfering with progress caused by physical barriers or obstacles placed in the way (as in, "most of the view was *obstructed* by billboards"). Go with block to imply *obstructing* passage or progress completely (as in, "a landslide blocked the road").

Write four sentences that show the correct way to use the words *hinder, impede, obstruct* and *block.* Use one of those words in each sentence.

_____
_____
_____
_____

3. *Meddling* is only one way to intrude on someone's life. Which one of the following words is a synonym of the word *meddle?*

    A. interpret
    B. interject
    C. interfere
    D. interrupt

Word History Detective:
The Case of One Unique Guy

There are good guys and bad guys. Which kind of guys gave English the word *guy?* Track down the original *guy* in the dictionary. Then write a paragraph that explains how the average fellow came to be called a *guy* in English.

© 2004 Merriam-Webster Inc.

Your name _____

Word Workout: Vocabulary Builder 15

1. Look up *spendthrift* in the dictionary. Then read the sentences below. Which sentence uses the word *spendthrift* correctly?

    A. Jade *spendthrift* ten dollars on a birthday gift for her Mom.
    B. You can tell Tim is a *spendthrift*—he just bought his tenth pair of shoes this month!
    C. That new French restaurant is too *spendthrift* for my budget.
    D. Lucy is a *spendthrift* who always saves her weekly allowance and puts in the bank.

2. Read the paragraph below. Then answer the question that follows.

Franz Anton Mesmer was an Austrian doctor in the late 1700s. He claimed that a mysterious fluid he called *animal magnetism* flowed through all matter. He had his patients sit in a tub of dilute acid and touch "magnetized" iron bars, and then he tapped them with a wand. Mesmer said the animal magnetism would flow from his body through the wand into the patient. Eventually it was discovered there was no flow of animal magnetism. The effects of the treatment were all in the patient's mind. Mesmer had discovered—or rediscovered—the techniques that we call **hypnotism**. *Mesmerize* is a synonym of *hypnotize,* and it can also mean "to fascinate."

Which conclusion below is best supported by the information in the paragraph?

    A. The word *magnetism* developed from the word *hypnotize.*
    B. The word *mesmerize* is older than the word *hypnotize.*
    C. The word *magnetism* is a synonym of the word *mesmerize.*
    D. The word *mesmerize* developed from the name of an Austrian doctor.

3. Read the sentence below. Look up the boldfaced word in your dictionary. Then answer the question that follows.

The book showed a picture of a lovely young queen wearing a beautiful golden crown *adorned* with sparkling diamonds, emeralds, and rubies.

Which word below could be used to replace *adorned* in the sentence above without changing the meaning of the sentence?

    A. embellished
    B. scorned
    C. spoiled
    D. attached

Word History Detective:
The Case of the Tunneling Terrier

Let a typical **terrier** loose, and chances are the dog will go racing all over the place, chasing leaves and squirrels and exploring every nook and cranny. Terriers are very active dogs. But why do we call them *terriers*? See if you can dig up the answer in your dictionary. Then write a paragraph telling how *terriers* got their name.

© 2004 Merriam-Webster Inc.

Answer Key
for How To Use Your Dictionary and How To Use Your Thesaurus

1. Alphabetical Order—Getting Started
Test Your Alphabet Skills
1. cat, dog, horse, mouse, pig
2. jaunt, lyric, sled, TV, umbrella
3. acrobat, lazy, noodle, octopus, vitamin

Test Your Alphabet Skills
1. bad, bike, blouse, boy, broccoli
2. seven, share, snap, store, sunny
3. icy, ignition, industry, irk, ivy

Test Your Alphabet Skills
1. chalk, cheese, chili, chop, chute
2. cannon, canopy, capable, capacious, capstan
3. draggle, dragnet, dragon, dragonfly, dragoon

2. Alphabetical Order—Moving Along
Test Your Alphabet Skills
1. figure of speech, figure out, fir, firecracker, fire escape
2. all-star, allude, any, anyone, anywise
3. double, double bass, doubleheader, double-jointed, double play
4. man, manage, management, manifold, man-made

Alphabet Investigator
First part of message: Alexis alleges alligators, dromedaries, elephants, foxes, hedgehogs, ibexes, jackals mysteriously vanished.
Second part of message: Concerned keepers near panic. Report to Toucan Tower.
Third part of message: Investigate suspect wearing white windbreaker with yellow zipper.

3. Guide Words
Test Your Guide Word Skills
(Guide words from *Merriam-Webster's Elementary Dictionary*)
1. cough • country
2. scrol • sea gull
3. offhand • old maid
4. messy • microcomputer
5. housework • humiliation
6. talk • tannin
7. ax • background
8. gamely • garment
9. collar • columbine
10. collar • columbine
11. shy • sieve
12. perch • perk
13. safe • sale
14. barge • base
15. bank • bargain
16. upstream • utensil
17. humility • hush-hush
18. humility • hush-hush
19. adjoin • adulterating
20. deplore • derrick

4. End-of-Line Divisions
Segmenting Words
1. em·per·or 2. snow·man 3. cray·on
4. ox·y·gen 5. piz·za 6. mis·con·duct
7. pa·ja·mas 8. as·ter·oid 9. ted·dy bear
10. ma·caw 11. teach·er 12. glob·al
13. zo·di·ac 14. im·per·son·al 15. pyr·a·mid
16. pick·er·el 17. platy·pus 18. obe·lisk
19. broth·er 20. re·la·tion·ship
21. ed·u·ca·tion 22. pome·gran·ate
23. im·por·tance 24. roy·al·ty 25. ori·ole

26. orang·utan 27. oc·ta·gon
28. tour·na·ment

5. Pronunciation
What's That Sound?
1. \ˈhənch\   2. i-ˈkäl-ə-jē
3. pər-ˈkəsh-ən   4. ˈsham-ˌräk
5. ˈzōd-ē-ˌak   6. ˈhī-bər-ˌnāt
7. fē-ˈes-tə   8. ˈyüs-fəl

What's That Word?
1. hot dog   \ˈhät-ˌdȯg\
2. fun   \ˈfən\
3. onion   \ˈən-yən\
4. imagination   \im-ˌaj-ə-ˈnā-shən\
5. fine   \ˈfīn\
6. apple   \ˈap-əl\
7. south   \ˈsau̇th\
8. fin   \ˈfin\
9. homework   \ˈhōm-ˌwərk\
10. fan   \ˈfan\
11. giant   \ˈjī-ənt\

6. More About Pronunciation
Find the Syllables
\ˈfā-və-rə-bəl\, \ˈdī-nə-ˌsȯr\, \ˈrən-ə-ˌwā\, \ˈau̇t-ˌpā-shənt\, \pə-ˈpī-ə\, \ri-ˈkȯrd-ər\, \ə-ˈpäl-ə-ˌjīz\, \ˈmaj-ə-stē\, \pə-ˈsif-ik\, \ˈtel-ə-ˌvizh-ən\

All Stressed Out
\ˈhäl-ə-ˌdā\, \ˈmag-ˌpī\, \ˈtüth-ˌbrəsh\, \ˌtäp-sē-ˈtər-vē\, \ˈkāt-ē-ˌdid\, \ˈfül-ˌhärd-ē\, \ˌpräb-ə-ˈbil-ət-ē\, \ˌsed-ə-ˈment-ə-rē\, \ˈwā-ˌsīd\, \ˌnav-ə-ˈgā-shən\

Putting It All Together
\ˈnā-vē\, \ˈtēn-ˌā-jər\, \tə-ˈlep-ə-thē\, \ə-ˈləm-nə\, \ˈmēt-ē-ər\, \ˈstrȯ-ˌber-ē\, \ˌev-rē-ˌdā\, \ˈlü-mə-nəs\, \ˈzōd-ē-ˌak\, \fə-ˈnal-ē\

7. Still More About Pronunciation
Be a Dictionary Detective
\ˈnərv-ˈfī-bər\, \ig-ˈzȯst\, \ik-ˈsting-gwish-ər\ \ˈstȯr-mē-nəs\, \kən-ˈklü-siv-lē\ \ˈman-ij-ər-ˌship\, \ˈī-ˌtēth\ \ˌau̇t-ˌbōrd-ˈmōt-ər\, \ˈfāth-fə-lē\, \ˈpled\

8. Variants
Variant or Misspelling?
Cross out: capitle, barnickle, calipper, ballust, garaje, poinsetta, peddlar, sinapse, ryme, riggorous, sirrup, insentive, barel

Which Is Preferred?
Circle: hooves, judgment, smelled, fungi, shod, oxen, vacuums, quartet, juncos, eerie, encrust, shrank, hurrah, hooray, hurrah, distill, among, biceps

9. Functional Labels
Birds of a Feather
vb: go, well, remember, succeed, brief, run, cloud
n: cloud, dictionary, computer, well, scorpion, run
adj: adorable, well, our, awful, brief
adv: anywhere, strangely, well, by, but
pron: these, she, you
conj: but, or, nor, and, because
prep: beside, between, into, by, because of, but
interj: ouch, well, hello, oh, hey

10. Homographs
Which Is Which?
First column: 1, 2, 1, 3, 2
Second column: 2, 1, 4, 2, 1

Two for the Price of One
1. fall, fall 2. fans, fan 3. right, right
4. base, base 5. tense, tense 6. can, can
7. light, light 8. expressed, express
9. low, low

11. Inflected Forms

Animals and Others

mantises, mantes; fungi, funguses; fezzes; dromedaries; tracheae; reindeer; fish, fishes; wolves; knives; flamingos, flamingoes; halves; quail, quails; chassis; geese; hooves, hoofs; octopuses, octopi

It Happened One Morning

woke, saw, heard, sang, came, scared, lay, took

Good, Better, Best

2. worse, worst   3. greener, greenest
4. happier, happiest   5. wryer, wryest
6. farther or further, farthest or furthest
7. zanier, zaniest   8. windier, windiest
9. fatter, fattest   10. smaller, smallest
11. narrower, narrowest
12. muddier, muddiest

12. Usage Labels

Getting It Right

1.c, 2.b, 3.c, 4.a, 5.b, 6.c,
7.b, 8.b, 9.c, 10.a, 11.a, 12.c

13. Definitions—Meaning

Look It Up

1.b, 2.b, 3.a, 4.d

Context Is Key

1.a, 2.c, 3.b

14. Definitions—Historical Order

Tried and True

1.c, 2.a, 3.c, 4.b

Cutting Edge

1.a, 2.c, 3.b, 4.c

15. Synonyms and Cross-references

Synonyms, Synonyms

produce, corridor, effect, fix, stocky, unimportant, regular, malted milk, privately, glimmer, hint, speck

One Step, Two Step

1.a, 2.c, 3.c, 4.a, 5.b

16. Verbal Illustration

Which Phrase Fits?

1.c, 2.a, 3.b, 4.a, 5.b, 6.b

Which Meaning Matches?

1.b, 2.c, 3.b, 4.c, 5.a, 6.c

17. Usage Notes

Usual Uses

1.b, 2.d, 3.c, 4.d

Using Usage

1.a, 2.c, 3.b, 4.c

18. Undefined Entries

Words Plus

4, 16, 9, 13, 20, 14, 1, 10, 3, 8, 23, 18, 24, 21, 12, 17, 7, 5, 2, 19, 6, 22, 15, 11

19. Synonym Paragraphs

Shades of Meaning

1. joy, pleasure, enjoyment
2. repair, patch, mend
3. tranquil, calm, peaceful
4. job, task, duty

20. Phrases

Eureka!

1. put 2. blue 3. take 4. spite 5. time
6. get 7. make 8. common 9. beside
10. contrary 11. turn 12. hand
13. play 14. follow 15. spot 16. mean

What Does It Mean?
1.c, 2.a, 3.a, 4.c, 5.b, 6.c, 7.c

21. Word History Paragraphs
Where in the World?
1. Greek 2. Arabic 3. French 4. Latin
5. Old English 6. Latin 7. Greek 8. Greek
9. Czech 10. Latin 11. German 12. French
13. Arabic 14. Latin 15. German 16. Dutch
17. Italian 18. Latin 19. Old English
20. Greek

Looking Back
3, 12, 4, 13, 18, 11, 16, 1, 6, 9, 17, 15,
5, 8, 14, 7, 2, 10

22. What Is a Thesaurus?
Find The Misfit
1. tawny 2. scrawl 3. saturate 4. idolize
5. identical 6. illumination 7. dexterous
8. ruthless

Dictionary Versus Thesaurus
1. yes 2. no 3. yes 4. no 5. yes 6. no
7. yes 8. yes 9. yes 10. yes

23. Meaning Cores and Verbal Illustrations
Matchmaker
5, 3, 7, 1, 4, 2, 6

Matchmaker
2, 6, 7, 1, 3, 5, 4

24. Synonyms and Related Words
Bet on a Set
1.b, 2.c, 3.b, 4.c, 5.c, 6.c

All in The Family
1.b, 2.a, 3.a, 4.a, 5.a

25. Phrases
One and the Same
First Column: 4, 15, 7, 8, 13
Second Column: 5, 14, 1, 10, 3
Third Column: 6, 9, 12, 11, 2

26. Antonyms and Contrasted Words
Find the Antonym
1.b, 2.c, 3.c, 4.a, 5.c, 6.b

Find the Near Antonym
1.c, 2.a, 3.c, 4.c, 5.b, 6.b

Opposites Attract
simplify—complicate
send—receive
mature—young
top—low
truth—fiction
approach—retreat
decrease—enlarge
pessimist—optimist
run—crawl
humid—dry
modern—old-fashioned

© 2004 Merriam-Webster Inc.

Answer Key
for Vocabulary Builder and Word History Exercises

This answer key includes both direct answers to questions and enrichment material teachers may elect to share with students. For open-ended questions, supporting material is included where possible to provide documentation to aid in assessing student responses.

Vocabulary Builder 1:

1. **B.** kid. **Enrichment:** *Banter* means to speak in a friendly but teasing or witty way. Other synonyms of banter include *joke, josh, razz, rag,* and *rib.*

2. Our teacher instructed us to write our names in all *capitals.*
   The encyclopedia says that Ottawa is the *capital* of Canada.
   The Chairman proposed investing some of the company's *capital* in computers.
   The governor is sworn in on the steps of the state *capitol.*
   Enrichment: The word *capitol* refers exclusively to the building in which a legislature meets. It is capitalized when it refers to the U.S. Capitol.

3. **A.** section. **Enrichment:** If you look closely, you'll see that an insect's body has segments, or sections. This makes insects look as though they have notches cut into them. That appearance led the ancient Greeks to call insects *entomon,* a name that came from their word *entomos,* meaning "cut up." Later, when the Romans wanted a word for this kind of creature, they translated *entomon* into the Latin word *insectum,* based on the Latin verb *insecare,* meaning "to cut into." English borrowed *insectum,* respelling it as *insect.* English also adopted the Greek *entomon,* which became the basis for the word *entomology,* meaning "the study of insects."

Word History Detective: Lily-livered: In the Middle Ages, doctors thought that four bodily fluids controlled a person's personality and health. Those fluids were blood, phlegm, black bile, and yellow bile. Medieval physicians also believed that you would demonstrate particular personality traits or health problems if you had too much or too little of one of those fluids in your system. They felt that yellow bile (also called *choler*) controlled anger and courage, and that if there wasn't enough choler in a person's system, his or her liver would turn white. Hence, a cowardly person was said to be *lily-livered.*

Vocabulary Builder 2:

1. **C.** In the word *emancipation* between lines 5 and 6.

2. **C.** conundrum. **Enrichment:** The words *mystery, enigma, puzzle,* and *conundrum* all name something that is hard to understand or explain. *Mystery* usually refers to something that cannot be fully understood by human reason or easily explained. (For example, "the *mystery* surrounding the building of ancient temples.") *Enigma* applies to words or actions that are very difficult to interpret correctly. (For example, "What she meant by her last remark is an *enigma.*") *Puzzle* applies to a tricky problem that challenges one to provide a solution. (For example, "It's a *puzzle* who took the chairs from the room and why.") *Conundrum* may apply to punning riddles or unsolvable problems inviting speculation. (For example, "the *conundrum* of which came first, the chicken or the egg.")

3. **B.** We traveled *incognito,* pretending to be Mr. and Mrs. John Smith.

Word History Detective: Eavesdropper: Imagine this: you're a medieval knight trying to find out if the king's advisors are plotting against you. You know the room where they are talking is guarded. Where could you safely hide to listen in to the conversation? Under the eaves. The eaves are the part of the roof of a house that hang over the wall, and an eavesdropper was literally someone who stood under the dripping eaves to hear a conversation. The original eavesdroppers may have just been looking for a place to stay dry and overheard conversations by accident. Later ones, though, were surely listening to others talk on purpose. We got the verb *eavesdrop* from the noun *eavesdropper,* and the word has been in strong use ever since.

Vocabulary Builder 3:

1. **D.** There were *copious* amounts of food at the party, and I tried all the goodies.

2. **B.** *Attribute* is pronounced one way when it is used as a noun and a different way when it is used as a verb.

3. **A.** skulking. **Enrichment:** The words *lurk, skulk,* and *sneak* all mean to move or act so as not to be noticed. *Lurk* suggests lying in wait usually with the intention of attacking (for example, "a fox *lurked* in the woods"). *Skulk* strongly suggests moving about quietly, often with an evil intention but sometimes in fear (for example, "a suspicious-looking person *skulking* about the grounds"). *Sneak* suggests moving into or out of a place in such a way as to avoid detection (for example, "*sneaked* into the kitchen and grabbed an apple").

Word History Detective: Guillotine: Joseph-Ignace Guillotin was a doctor and supporter of the French Revolution. Guillotin felt that all death sentences associated with the Revolution should be carried out by beheading, a punishment formerly reserved for nobles. He also believed that, for humane reasons, a machine should be used for the executions. One such machine had already been perfected by a German mechanic named Schmitt under the supervision of another French doctor, Antoine Louis. At first the execution machine was called the *Louison* or *Louisette.* But a royalist sympathizer suggested changing the name to *guillotine,* probably because Dr. Guillotin was better known than Dr. Louis.

Vocabulary Builder 4:

1. **C.** His moods change quickly and unpredictably.

2. **D.** to throw in the way of. **Enrichment:** *Obicere* means "to throw in the way of." When a person objects to something, they are throwing their opinion in the way of the thing they object to. *Obicere* itself comes from the Latin verb *jacere* that means "to throw"; that latter verb has also given English *eject* (literally, "to throw away"), *project* ("to throw before or in front of"), and *reject* ("to throw backwards or away from oneself").

3. **A.** going on vacation. **Enrichment:** In David Copperfield by Charles Dickens, David describes another character as "brooding so long that I could not decide whether to run the risk of disturbing him by going, or to remain quietly where I was, until he should come out of his reverie." This passage shows how *reverie* implies daydreaming or deep thought that can block out awareness of anything else. English took *reverie* from a French word meaning "to wander," and wander is what our minds do when we are in reverie.

Word History Detective: Grotesque: Italians digging among the ruins of ancient Rome found strange paintings on the walls of some of the rooms. These paintings were of human and animal forms mixed with those of strange fruits and flowers. Italians called such a painting *pintura grottesca,* which means "cave painting." The word *grottesca* came from the Italian

© 2004 Merriam-Webster Inc.

grotta, meaning "cave." (The English *grotto,* another word for "cave," also came from the Italian *grotta. Grotta*, in turn, came from *crypta,* the Latin word for a cavern or crypt.) The French turned the Italian adjective *grottesca* into *grotesque,* the form in which it came into English. At first, the English adjective was used to describe pictures having strange combinations of things not normally found together. Later it came to be used for anything that looked weird or unnatural.

Vocabulary Builder 5:

1. **A.** To keep her homework organized, Isabel used *discrete* sections in her notebook for each subject.
   B. The coach was always very *discreet*, refusing to discuss why a player didn't make the team.
   C. Each lab partner was instructed to complete a *discrete* step in the experiment.
   D. Although Kevin and Kyle were twins, they had very different personalities and *discrete* interests.

2. **C.** It comes from the name of a stingy French government official. **Enrichment:** Etienne de Silhouette served as the French controller general of finances in 1759. He became noted for being extremely stingy with the government's money. He would not allow any unnecessary expenses and reduced government pensions. People began making fun of his overly strict regulations for saving money. It was said that he was so cheap that he decorated his walls with cutout outline drawings instead of real paintings. Such outline or profile drawings eventually came to be called by his name, *silhouettes.*

3. **B.** cows. **Enrichment:** Toward the end of the 18th century, English physician Edward Jenner observed that dairymaids who had had the disease cowpox did not contract the much more serious disease smallpox. Working from this observation, Jenner injected a person with material taken from someone else's cowpox sores. He discovered that the injection protected the second person against smallpox. When he reported these findings in an article, he called cowpox by its Latin name, *variolae vaccinae.* The Latin word *vaccinae* was formed from the adjective *vaccinus,* meaning "of or relating to cows." This word, in turn, was based on the noun *vacca,* meaning "cow." The cowpox material used for original injections was dubbed *vaccine* and the injection itself was called a *vaccination.* From this noun we created the verb *vaccinate* and the noun *vaccinator.*

Word History Detective: Buccaneer: In the 17th century, French hunters living in the West Indies were known as *boucaniers.* They were given that name because they used the native Indian method of preserving meat by smoking it over a wooden grill. The grill was called a *boucan,* after the Brazilian Indian name for it. Pirates operating in this area used the same method of preserving meat, so they came to be called *buccaneers,* the English spelling of the French *boucaniers.* Some synonyms of *buccaneer* are *pirate, corsair, freebooter, picaroon, rover, sea dog, sea robber,* and *sea rover.*

Vocabulary Builder 6:

1. **D.** A man who pays too much attention to his clothes. **Enrichment:** The word *dude* has had an active life since it appeared during the late 1800s to refer to a man overly concerned with the way he dresses. Soon after that, *dude* was born again, this time as a city dweller unfamiliar with life on the range, especially an Easterner in the Wild West. In the late 1930s, *dude* evolved into a synonym for *guy.* Its next big move was into surfer slang, used as a

term of address or as a descriptive noun applied to a fellow surfer. Never quite dying out in the 1970s, *dude* resurfaced in the 1980s and lives on in teen slang today.

2. **A.** I like to read so I *frequent* the library.
   B. Jamie *frequently* uses the phone to call her friends.
   C. Mr. Allen *frequently* golfs in his spare time.
   D. Our grandparents visit our house *frequently*.

3. **Open ended. Enrichment:** The words *rebuke, reprimand, admonish,* and *chide* all mean to express criticism of. *Rebuke* suggests a severe or stern criticism. (For example, "He *rebuked* the students for bad conduct at the game.") *Reprimand* suggests a formal and often public or official rebuke. (For example, "The general was *reprimanded* by the President for an unwise speech.") *Admonish* suggests an earnest or friendly warning or piece of advice. (For example, "We were *admonished* for talking too loud.") *Chide* suggests a mild scolding that expresses displeasure or disappointment. (For example, "My parents *chided* me for my table manners.")

Word History Detective: Bunk: *Bunk* is a shortened version of *bunkum* or *buncombe*. According to a story that has become part of American political folklore, the phrase "talk to bunkum" originated around 1820, when Felix Walker, a U.S. Congressman from Buncombe County, North Carolina, gave a very long speech despite the protests of his impatient colleagues. In his own defense, Walker explained he had done what his constituents expected of him, which was "to make a speech for Buncombe." Whether this story is true or not, it gave rise to the words *bunkum* and *bunk*.

Vocabulary Builder 7:

1. **B.** pebbles. **Enrichment:** In Latin *calculus* meant "pebble." Because the Romans used pebbles to do addition and subtraction on a counting board, the word became associated with computation. The English word *calculate* comes ultimately from the Latin *calculus*. The word *calculus* has also been borrowed into English as a medical term to refer to hard masses in the body, such as kidney stones, which resemble pebbles.

2. **D.** *aequus* means "equal" and *nox* means "night."

3. **Open ended.** Student answers may vary based on their interpretation of information in the paragraph given in the exercise.

Word History Detective: Tabby: A silk cloth with a striped pattern was once made in part of the city Baghdad in what is now the country of Iraq. The Arabic name for the cloth was 'attabi, from Al-'Attabiya, the name of the part of the city where it was made. A version of the Arabic word was borrowed into Latin, and later the French adapted the Latin name for the cloth into their language, calling it *tabis*. When English speakers adopted the word, they turned it into *tabby*. People saw a resemblance between the striped or wavy pattern of the silk cloth and the striped or spotted markings on the fur of some cats. Cats with markings like the cloth came to be called *tabby cats* or just *tabbies*.

Vocabulary Builder 8:

1. **D.** On our expedition to the woods, we found a new path we had never seen before.
2. **C.** The sentence uses both the noun *console* and the verb *console* correctly.
3. **A.** onomatopoeia

Word History Detective: Boycott: In 1880, there were many crop failures in Ireland. A famine seemed likely, and the tenants on the farm estates were not able to pay their rents in full. The tenants of one estate asked the estate manager, Charles Boycott, to lower the rents to a level they could pay. He refused and tried to have them evicted from the property. As a result, the tenants refused to work for him. They went further, and forced Boycott's servants to leave him, stopped his mail and food deliveries, and even threatened his life. In short, they made his life wretched without using violence. This treatment of Boycott was reported in the papers, and when other tenants used the same treatment against their estate managers, it was called a *boycott* action. The term gained popularity, and today we use *boycott* as a noun and a verb.

Vocabulary Builder 9:

1. **D.** Bud and Joey had a *vehement* debate about whose soccer team is best.

2. **D.** handle. **Enrichment:** The words *handle*, *manipulate*, and *wield* mean to manage skillfully or efficiently. *Handle* suggests applying an acquired skill in order to accomplish something. (For example, "She knows how to *handle* her bike well.") *Manipulate* suggests using special skills in order to accomplish a complicated or difficult task. (For example, "Surgeons must be able to *manipulate* delicate instruments.") *Wield* suggests handling a tool or weapon with power or authority. (For example, "*wielded* the sword with all his might.")

3. **D.** rank. **Enrichment:** The words *putrid*, *rank*, and *musty* all mean "bad-smelling." *Putrid* implies particularly the sickening odor of decaying organic matter. (For example, "the *putrid* smell of rotting fish.") *Rank* suggests a strong unpleasant smell. (For example, "*rank* cigar smoke.") *Musty* suggests a lack of fresh air and sunlight and stresses the effects of dampness, mildew, or age. (For example, "the *musty* odor of a damp cellar.")

Word History Detective: Khaki: *Khaki* is one of a number of words, including *cot* and *shampoo*, that are by-products of British rule in India. The Hindi word *khaki*, meaning "dust-colored," was borrowed into English as a name for the color of a particular uniform cloth favored by British soldiers in India in the mid-1800s. *Khaki* is still used to name certain military uniforms, but nowadays English speakers also use it more generically for any clothes that have the dusty yellowish-brown color named by the Hindi ancestors *khaki*.

Vocabulary Builder 10:

1. **C.** In the sentence, *cocoon* is a verb meaning "to wrap yourself up tightly."

2. **C.** The English word *coward* developed from the French word *coart*.

3. **B.** ordinary and familiar **Enrichment:** The words *common*, *ordinary*, and *familiar* mean "occurring regularly and not in any way special, strange, or unusual." *Common* implies usual everyday quality or frequency of occurrence. (For example, "a *common* error.") It may additionally suggest inferiority or coarseness. (For example, "Their manners were quite *common*.") *Ordinary* stresses conformance in quality or kind with the regular order of things. (For example, "an *ordinary* pleasant summer day.") *Familiar* stresses the fact of being generally known and easily recognized. (For instance, "a *familiar* melody.")

Word History Detective: Date: The word *date* that means "the fruit of the palm" and the word *date* that means "the time of an event" look alike. They are not related to each other, though. And neither one is related to the word *day*. The word for the fruit can be traced back to the Greek word *daktylos*, originally meaning "finger" and "toe." No one knows just how the fruit came to be called by a word for finger. It may be because of its small size and shape or

© 2004 Merriam-Webster Inc.

because of the long slender shape of the palm leaves. Or it may be that this word *daktylos* was the closest Greek word to the sound of a word for the fruit borrowed from another language. The *date* meaning "the time of an event" derives from the Latin phrase *data Romae,* meaning "given at Rome," an expression used just before the date on letters and documents. The word *data* is from the Latin word *dare* "to give." In later Latin, the word *data* came to be used alone to stand for the date, and it came into English as *date.*

Vocabulary Builder 11:

1. **A.** The book was *ostensibly* written in the future to make the story seem more real.
2. **A.** Spanish ➔ French ➔ English.
3. **D.** *wood* and *sound.*

Word History Detective: Influenza: Originally the Italian word *influenza* meant what the similar-sounding word in English, *influence*, means today: "the act or power of producing an effect indirectly." But *influenza* also had the Latin meaning of "an invisible fluid through which the stars and planets control and direct the earth and things and people on it." When epidemics raged through Europe, no one knew what the real cause was. People blamed them on evil stars working through that mysterious invisible fluid. For this reason, the Italians called such diseases *influenza*. In 1743 an epidemic of an illness very much like modern influenza began in Rome and spread through Europe. That was when the Italian word was borrowed into English. *Flu* is a shortened form of *influenza*.

Vocabulary Builder 12:

1. **A.** Greg was *demure* when he won the prize, telling everyone he didn't deserve it.
2. **Open ended.** Student answers may vary.
3. **D.** to solve by thought or by clever guessing

Word History Detective: Pupil: If you look into another person's eye, you can see a small reflection of yourself. That small image in another's eye made the ancient Romans think of a tiny doll. Thus, they called the part of the eye in which it appears the *pupilla,* from a Latin word that literally meant "little doll." The English word for that part of the eye, *pupil,* can be traced to the Latin *pupilla*. *Pupilla* also had another meaning. A little girl who was an orphan and was in the care of a guardian was called a *pupilla*. A little boy in the same situation was called a *pupillus*. From these two Latin words we get the other English *pupil*, meaning "a young student in the care of a tutor or in school."

Vocabulary Builder 13:

1. **C.** moving or acting in a lazy, slow, or tired manner : loafing
2. **A.** recompense.
3. **B.** small, miniature

Word History Detective: Tantalize: Poor Tantalus! The mythical Greek king offended the gods, so he was condemned to eternal punishment in Hades. Tantalus was forced to stand up to his chin in water, but whenever he lowered his head to drink, the water receded so he couldn't reach it. When he stretched up to pick delicious fruit from the trees overhead, the branches moved out of his reach, so he remained hungry. Tantalus was always tormented by things he could see but not have, so English speakers made his name into a verb that describes the same kind of unfulfilled desire he suffered.

Vocabulary Builder 14:

1. **A.** composed

2. **Open ended.** Student answers may vary.

3. **C.** interfere. **Enrichment:** The words *meddle, interfere,* and *tamper* mean to concern oneself with something that is not one's own business. *Meddle* stresses intruding in a thoughtless and annoying fashion. (For example, "*meddling* in a friend's personal problems.") *Interfere* suggests getting in the way of or disturbing someone or something whether intentionally or not. (For example, "Your noise is *interfering* with my studying.") *Tamper* suggests intruding or experimenting that is wrong or uncalled-for and likely to be harmful. (For example, "They *tampered* with the lock in an effort to get into the building.")

Word History Detective: Guy: November 5 is a holiday in England that is celebrated by setting off fireworks and lighting bonfires. Human likenesses made of tattered clothes stuffed with hay or rags are burned on the bonfires. The holiday, called Guy Fawkes Day, is named for Guy Fawkes (1570-1606), a man who played a leading role in a historic plot to blow up the British Parliament buildings. Fawkes managed to hide 20 barrels of gunpowder in the cellars of the buildings. However, the plot was discovered before he could carry out his plans. He was seized and later put to death. The human likenesses burned to commemorate the failure of Guy Fawkes's plot came to be called *guys.* The use of the word was extended to similar figures and later to a person of strange appearance or dress. In the United States the word came to be used generally for any man, and in time it came to be used for a person of either sex.

Vocabulary Builder 15:

1. **B.** You can tell Tim is a *spendthrift*—he just bought his tenth pair of shoes this month!

2. **D.** The word *mesmerize* developed from the name of an Austrian doctor.

3. **A.** embellished. **Enrichment:** *Embellish, beautify, adorn,* and *decorate* all mean to improve the appearance of a thing by adding something that isn't essential. *Embellish* suggests the adding of unnecessary details. (For example, "Our dishes are *embellished* with a leaf design.") *Beautify* stresses the improvement of something plain. (For example, "New flower boxes *beautify* the street.") *Adorn* suggests that the thing added is beautiful in itself. (For example, "A gold star *adorned* the tree.") *Decorate* often refers to adding color or design to something that is a bit dull. (For example, "Silvio *decorated* his room with posters.")

Word History Detective: Terrier: Today most terriers are kept as pets. However, there was a time when the dogs were widely used for hunting. Terriers are usually small dogs with short legs, and they were used to dig game animals such as foxes, badgers, and weasels out of their holes or burrows. The dogs were also trained to go into a hole after a game animal and drive it out. English speakers borrowed the word *terrier* from the French name for these dogs, *chien terrier,* which literally means "earth dog." The French name can be traced back to the Latin word *terra,* meaning "earth."